The Dreaming Well

Reclaiming and Working with the Spirits of the Depths,
And the Mythology of the Wild in Dreaming, Story and Song

Travis Wernet

"Have you been touched by the Spirit of the Land? It's inside every woman and inside every man, from a far away call into the palm of your hand, it's time to know and listen, to look and understand."

Spirit of the Land, Liam O'Maonlai, Hothouse Flowers

Dedicated to all the Dreamers and Teachers, many-rooted, several-footed, wild of hair and heart who have helped shape this offering through curious and devoted learning and sharing amid the grief-laden days and nights of our lives, that, with effort and attention also yield the unlikely fruits of wonder and joyfulness who always find their way through despite our hopes and fears. With a special wind of gratitude to Mardi for true and devoted support for this mighty effort.

In Love, Trust and Graciousness, Travis Wernet

Table of Contents

Introduction Pt 1 – A Gaze Into the Well pg 7

Ch 1 – How Do We Know What We Don't Know? Pg 17

Ch 2 – Apocalypse Again, the Vast Healing Potential of Dreams pg 44

Ch 3- This Darkness is the Lighthouse pg 85

Ch 4 – Mythic Embodiments, the Roots of Life's Projects pg 121

Ch 5 – Skeleton Woman pg 133

Ch 6 – Sifting Among the Bones pg 141

Introduction Pt 2 – Dream Songs on the Road of Life and Death pg 201

Ch 7- Sound, Dreams, Soul and Spiritpg 219

Ch 8 – Ancient and Contemporary Dream Incubation pg 248

Acknowledgements

Big and heart-felt thanks to my loving and creative partner Mardi
for all her patience and support and influence on this work. I'd also
very much like to thank Jeremy Taylor for years worth of gracious
and soulful, wise instruction and assistance, as well as kind
friendship and mentoring. Here's to Michael Meade for close and
distant, adept and genius mentoring and also to Martin Shaw for
helping to bring the language of the wild into eloquent and blood-
filled life within and without. My deepest gratitude goes as well to
Marilyn Geist, canny and devoted aid, and to Aubrey Degnan,
loving friend and teacher. I have to also acknowledge my family,
alive and dead, two-legged and four-legged (!) who have assisted
and informed this work through waking moments too numerous to
detail and also via dreams, where the mysteries of connection may
become more clear as we sleep at night. A final tip of the hat to the
Wild , the Cultured and to All Our Relations through time who
continue to instruct, feed and beguile.

Introduction
A Gaze Into the Well

Dreams appear to us such that we speak of how they come from within. One of the greatest benefits we may draw from our dreams has to do with this fact, no matter how we describe it or explain it. Inner messages, experiences and visions which occur to us while we're asleep or in states of reverie, trance, hunches, bodily sensations and flights of imagination are all part of the tapestry of the garment we might refer to as *the Dreaming*. We even describe the visions and aspirations we have for our lives by speaking of dreams.

There are a multitude of ways to seek to learn from and work alongside the wilding creative forces of the soul in pursuit of an immersed awareness of the wisdom that comes from beyond what we know as waking personalities and our conscious – that is to say, 'known' - life understandings. It's been my experience time and again that all approaches, from the more feeling-based to the more thinking-influenced and on to the attempts to *stay with the image* and somatic or body-oriented paths towards honoring dreams, have something vital and important to offer. All the major and minor efforts at seeking to honor visionary experiences have something truthful to give us.

The many domains of dreaming can be seen to be as immense as waking life tends to be. Possibly even more so, due to the apparently limitless, deeper, more mysterious quality of the realms where dreams take place and originate from. Any effort to describe dreaming forays in language or art will tend to fall short when compared to the actual perceptions, feelings and experiences we have in the dreaming worlds. This is no reason not to seek to share, explore and learn from our dreams. Interpretation, to a point, has been of great value to myself, and numerous folks whom I've worked with. A cross-cultural review of dreaming cultures throughout time reveals this is also true for a diverse bevy of dream explorers from Native American Iroquois peoples to ancient Greek students of the Dreaming and beyond.

One of the major invitations of our imaginal flights is to find a way to ferry energies back and forth between what has been called the conscious and the unconscious, the known and the unknown, the waking physical world and the non-ordinary dream world. As poet David Whyte says in his poem, *What to Remember When Waking*, "to remember the other world in this world is to live your true inheritance". At the same time, it does appear to be helpful to remember that in using the tools available to us, we are usually only approximating the depth, height, bewilderment and utter magnificence of the wildly diverse energies who present themselves in dreams.

Making music and sound, noticing it as it appears in the spaces around us, is an attention to the Invisibles, those who are *not seen*. There are at least as many expressions of sound available to us, as there are states of being, acting, thinking and feeling. Music and sound have long held the intrigue of our human and spiritual, soulful regards. I think this is because of their capacious tendency to pull together universal yet inviolably personal colors, threads and intuitions, emotions, felt-experiences and living sensations.

Attendants of music and sound have long spoken of the ways that expressive arts open us to important layers of full-blooded and whole-spirited existences. It is truly as if a blessing occurs when certain kinds of sound are invoked. The very word *blessing*, from the French "blesseur", originally referred to a kind of opening up to the divine. An old idea of blessing was variously understood as an occurrence of meeting *larger-than-life energies* and being influenced by them. Being blessed even meant being wounded so that relation could be made between the human and the sacred. That may be why wounds are also openings. Some blessings are requested and others arrive unbidden.

A true blessing tends to occur for each of us when we are suffering from an overly imbalanced sense of how everything seems to depend upon our isolated human energies. When we forget that there's more to life than meets the eye, and that there are more energies in life, death, the day, the night and the cosmos than merely human ones, openings sometimes appear where the divine necessarily breaks through to remind us of how things actually are.

In our dreams bewildering events of benediction might take the form of nightmares. In the realm of sound, it might be a thunderclap or a mighty wind, a certain instrument or sung lyric that suddenly reaches out and rends or buoys our hearts. It might even be a song that overwhelms us with its ability to express a precision of essence evoked through the tones of a beguiling melody. The more we tend our relationship to the sacred, the less surprised we may be by the archetypal energies of Great Nature and the Divine. It's not that the unexpected never arrives, but more like when it does, at least the ability to dance with it has also been attempted and practiced.

Poetry and storytelling, forms of spoken sound in which words are crafted to evoke vital truths can also act upon us as an untamed form of epiphanic rupturing and sustenance. Through soulful language and feeling, image and symbol, well-honed words bear a potency for regaining our core selves. Through artful language, we may also come to recognize our place within a multi-faceted cosmos that includes cornucopias of well-furred animals, fancifully feathered birds, swaying trees, swelling oceans, solidifying earths and beclouded skies.

Art itself, much more than the literal forms we may have come to identify it with, when fully embodied and at its most spontaneous, brings about the creative-destructive spirit of living and dying. All amid the strains of Underworld energies, human longings and the well-rumored Great Beyond. We humans have made artistic utterances since time immemorial exactly because the soul in us and in the world longs to give voice to the clarifying yet mystical beauties, the remembrances and tragedies of being and belonging. Something in us is compelled to bring forth imaginative creations that have the ability to move, stir, embolden, break open and revitalize us. Such evocations do not, when authentically rendered, diminish who we are, they confirm our truest senses of identity amid a living cosmos.

There may be no more vibrant source for drawing upon and relating to these energies of originality, the sources of our origins, than the wellsprings of our dreams. Think upon the collection of dreams that you have played a part within and witnessed during your own lifetime. Simply marvel at their unbridled tendency to put actions, elements, people and situations together that don't seem to fit or make sense, except within the context of the dreams themselves. And yet, these things do occur while we're asleep, and make sense *in the dreaming*. And so, such occasions are real while we're dreaming and sleeping, at the very least.

Mythologists and students of Fairy Tales have widely spoken of the interconnections between archetypal narratives and dreams. Joseph Campbell called dreams "personal myths" and myths "public dreams". Marie-Louise Von Franz has spoken in many of her writings about the likelihood that folk tales originate from dreams that get passed around among many pairs of hands and are uttered by a multitude of musical, faithful tongues and mouths. Akin to what storyteller Martin Shaw says about "what's happening now", we seem to be entering a time where we can allow the symbols to live within us and our selves to live within them, rather than bend them to endless psychological or intellectual theorizing. As Shaw puts it, we appear to be entering the realization that *we are living in the stories themselves*, rather than the other way round.

When creators have turned to their dreams, we've received a wealth of boons bearing innovation, power and wonder. Everything from Einstein's Theory of Relativity and the immensely famous song "Yesterday", the Google search engine and on to the modern sewing needle, have been forged out of the inventive-creative-revelatory spaces of dreams. This has also occurred in a myriad of influential works in literature, folklore, mythology and timeless poems. *Frankenstein* as well as *Dr. Jekyll and Mr. Hyde*, to name a couple famous cultural artifacts of the past few hundred years, have come to us out of the storied land of dreaming and continue to live well-fleshed existences.

Dreams, poems, art, great stories and music have their own way of getting right to the heart of matters and also shining forth a mighty elaboration of spiraling significances and truths that become timeworn for their depth of guidance. These wonderfully human and equally more-than-human creations also help to bring us out of the abstract. By so doing, such energies are brought into a breadth of relationship, allowing us to apprentice ourselves to crucial truths and soulful meanderings. These resplendent curiosities become tools for us to shake up our ordinary everyday awareness enough to remind us that life is an adventure and that we are essentially all still students in the greatest classroom on earth.

The Dreaming Well is one more in a long line of efforts at providing some guidance for ways to learn from and work with these wily and often bemusing, confounding forces to be found in our dreams and in the imagination. The task here is to provide a modest yet spiraling road map for approaching the dreams themselves with a set of runes so to speak, for divining the ability to try the ideas herein out for yourself. So many books exist that describe theoretical approaches or hard and fast rules about how to work with dreams. They may all be "right", but because dreams are so profound and since we as a culture here in the West dropped the art of dream work (for the most part) along the way, theoretical constructs and certain schools can tend to obscure the very subject which they seek to elucidate. Dreams provide direction and yet, they are also great mysteries to be respected, with the same honorifics one tends to be invited to approach the enormous wilding elementals of Great Nature itself.

My trust and devotion, then, is to attempt to expand upon a model for *starting with the dreams* and then asking the questions that might be the most helpful towards creating a space for them to show us their deeper and sometimes loftier or more humble, paradoxical truths. I have test-driven the insights shared in this book for the past twenty years, so I do feel that you'll very likely find some benefit and heft within what is being offered. I've also worked with a wide variety of folks from divergent walks of life and have found that most have benefitted enormously from these tools and perspectives. Several of the methods hail from my waking life teachers and from other quarters, including ancient peoples, and I will do my best to point out these sources along the way.

None of these ideas or insights will be of ultimate value to you unless you find that they hold a good place in your very own hearth. The encouragement I would suggest is to treat these offerings as garments you're trying on to see if they fit well or not. Sometimes it takes awhile to come around to a new style, so I also ask that you pay special attention to times when you might be strongly disagreeing with the notions here, as it tends to be true that the more allergic to a certain idea we are, the stronger the likelihood that we might hold a level of resistance towards it, because it's exactly the thing that we need to learn and understand. What seems foreign or even repellant can be and often is the 'missing piece' of the puzzle.

May the teachings, tales, sounds, ideas and creative approaches gathered here lead and nurture you, our world and many others to deeper levels of soulfulness, for the wholeness of your own being and that of all the leaping, feathered creatures and the greening, pulsing, living, dying, birthing denizens of this earth and the otherworlds to be found in the Dreaming as well as in the intersections between them.

Blessed Be, Travis Wernet, Occidental California, May 2016

CHAPTER 1

How Do We Know What We Don't Know?

"Many tribal peoples…preferred to call it… in their own languages…
the 'great mysterious'… the 'great holy'."
Vine Deloria Jr.

During the course of any sun-streaked day, beneath the starry expanse of any night, if we pause momentarily to reflect, we may realize that, as we turn to an acknowledgement of the fullness of the living world nearby, there is much that we are not aware of. Life and the cosmos are much larger and more expansive than our focused, limited, time-bound attentions usually allow us to recognize.

Like all that lives and exists within the mighty oceans and spacious skies that daily bless our efforts to craft a two-legged existence here on the ever-faithful terra firma, *there is much that we don't know that we don't know*. What's happening out there in deep space as you read these words? Who's out in those heaving marine swells as the earth makes its spinning orbit around the sun? Where is the moon at this very moment? What forms of life and mineral seethe and pulse beneath our very feet as we are held upon the earth?

There are many unknown realities taking place, at the same time that we are cognizant of what seems to be happening in our vicinity. In some very observable ways we simply don't appear able to perceive all the myriads of living processes occurring at a given moment. In other instances, we may have once been aware of a whole host of realities that we have forgotten or become unaware of, or simply haven't known as yet.

As Carl Jung put it in referring to his notion of an *autonomous objective source of being*, or, what I'm calling 'what we don't know that we don't know',

> "…the unconscious contains everything that is psychic that has not reached the threshold of consciousness… whose energy-charge is not sufficient to maintain it in consciousness, or… will reach consciousness in the future."[1]

Sometimes referred to as "the unconscious" and others as "the objective psyche", this domain can be understood as the realm where what is not known resides. Another way of speaking about unconsciousness might be to call it "the unknown".

Who amongst us hasn't undergone the annoyance of misplacing some seemingly unimportant item, like our house keys, due to the competing forces of attention vying for our limited awareness? More dramatically, how many of us can honestly say that we recall the day we were born into this life? A much bigger question of memory might be to ask whether we know where we were before we came here to be in these now familiar physical bodies. If we can't even remember the day we were born, what makes us so sure that we don't possess eternal souls or spirits that may have been off someplace else prior to this so-called incarnation?

Such are the questions of philosophy - the love of wisdom - and psychology –the deep knowledge and word of the soul - as well as of various spiritual traditions that have sought to undertake the task of seeking knowledge about why it is that we are here in the first place and what it all might mean to be born, to live, to die, to love, to create and to dream.

Because the unconscious, or we could say "the not-yet-speech-ripe", is composed of what we don't know 'in the moment', it's always worth stepping back and considering the possibility of surprising meanings in our dreams as well as in the events of our waking lives. When I say "not-yet-speech-ripe", I mean *that in us and in waking and dream worlds which is in existence, but which is far enough below or beyond the surface of awareness that we can't even speak about it, because it's not fully formed and we're remembering it or it's in the process of coming into awareness.* A well-known and oft-repeated quip of Jung's has it that, "The problem with the unconscious is that it *really is* unconscious". No matter how conscious we become, there is *always* the potential that we don't know what we don't know. How can we know what we don't know, if we don't know that we don't know it?

The term, not-yet-speech-ripe, comes to us from what Jeremy Taylor refers to as "the Anglo-Saxon word horde". This is really another way of speaking about, and perhaps a more poetic reference to what Jungians have called unconsciousness.

> "The old Anglo-Saxon term for 'unconscious' is *not-yet-speech-ripe*. Those things that our dreams are inviting us to see are not yet sufficiently conscious to be put into words. When someone else puts some of these potential insights into words, the dreamer consciously remembers, for the first time, what he or she already knew unconsciously..."[2]

Jung himself seems to have gone to great lengths to elucidate what he meant by this idea of that in us and outside of us which makes surprising appearances in our dreams and comes forth in unexpected revelations while we're awake. These are energies, which hold a vast memory of human and more-than-human instinctual experiences that arise out of the cauldron of psychic soul existence. In his work, Jung designates various levels of the unconscious, noting that there are a variety of characteristics to the energetic forces of the psyche that are vital to our understanding and being.

In dreams this model of awareness may show up in the imaginal form of a building with ever-descending structures trailing down below the surface from the ground floor. The further down one goes, the less familiar are the people, animals, beings and scenarios that present themselves. There are many dreams on record in the veritable wealth of literature on this topic that contain just such symbolic metaphors and depictions of psychic existence. I've seen many like this in my own recalling and that of folks I've worked with.

In terms of these various levels, there is what we call *the personal unconscious*. This is the storehouse of memories, feelings, thoughts and sensations that we develop within this lifetime. Try as we might, it appears impossible to be fully aware of all the perceptions and experiences we've had along the way. Much contemporary therapeutic psychology has been an effort to understand and work with the material that goes into and relates with this personal historical reservoir of memory and experience.

Central to Jung's practical theories, the approach to the soul known as Analytical Psychology, is the further notion of *the collective unconscious*. This is the psychic soul-force in the cosmos, which contains experiences and feelings, images and memories that are seen to be *transpersonal* and *universal*. The evidence for this mysterious yet engaging reality is closely linked to instinct and what we call archetypes. These realities can be witnessed quite readily in our dreams.

WINDOWS ONTO WHAT WE DON'T YET KNOW

There appears to be a force in nature that energetically instructs, guides and directs and which simply is. Our dreams are an invaluable source of such material when and where they can be seen to present us with symbols, situations, images, feelings and thoughts, that cannot be identified as having originated out of direct personal waking experience in this lifetime. Myths, folk and fairy tales as well as spiritual-religious visions also evince the existence of the collective unconscious, the beyond-personal not-yet-speech-ripe, in their thematic representations of repeating, human and earthly, yet also divinely wrought, cosmic images, energies, situations and scenarios. Dreams and stories bear a close connection.

In a big way, Nature is understandable as the Cosmos – the All That Is. We can talk about both as a broader context for our existence, within which is cradled the very human construct of culture. At the edges and boundaries of any culture, we find what we call *wilderness*. In his phenomenal book on Storytelling, the Ecstatic and Initiation, *A Branch From the Lightning Tree* storyteller Martin Shaw beseeches us,

"The mythology of wilderness needs to be articulated as the mythology of ourselves."[3]

Wilderness is another aspect of and metaphor about, as well as an actual reality that evokes "the Unknown". If we take Shaw's statement as truthful, and if you can accept my extension of it here, we may see how what we don't know belongs within as well as without. The wilderness as mythology, that is to say as *knowledge of story,* exists within as well as without. And it wants to be articulated, spoken.

Think of the time in our not too distant history when people in the West thought that the world was flat. People didn't know how the earth was actually shaped on a larger than immediately observable level, that planet earth as we understand it today, is a great spherical orb dancing a spiraling jig through the heavens. So convinced by the notion that the world was flat, some folks were willing to burn others to death at the stake for merely suggesting things might be otherwise!

We may look back, with supposedly enlightened and much wiser views, and say how foolish these people were, accepting and conceiving of the world as a flat disc. And yet, what is it that we ourselves today do not know now? What might people discover or remember in the future, that may become common knowledge, which we do not yet possess the ability to understand because it has not yet become speech-ripe? What lays there, just around the next bend on the trail, in the wilderness of the soul and out there in the world, the cosmos?

Dreams, in my view, are one of the best windows for looking onto what it is that we don't yet know that we don't know. When dreaming, we enter much more complete realities that have much to unveil to our curious souls, sleeping bodies, drumming hearts and searching minds.

> Taylor imparts,
> "A deeper encounter with dreams and myths can nurture creative imagination, creative self-realization and expression, compassion, and courage in ways that no other attention can achieve; and these are, as they have always been, the qualities and energies we need to confront our eternal human predicament."[4]

As a number of archaic peoples have known, for thousands of years, dreams reveal distinct levels of reality, wisdom and experience that transcend, yet deepen and include our ordinary, everyday human tendencies. In modern times, we have verified this through scientific means, and new casts have been crafted to describe long-held understandings. As we've noted, Carl Jung called the place dreams originate from the collective unconscious. Ancients from Ireland to Africa on to Iceland and Australia have spoken of this wellspring of knowledge and experience as *the Otherworld, the Spirit Realm* and *the Dreaming.*

No matter what we call it, there is a real and engagingly alive source that reveals visionary experiences to us. Here lies the territory of "the mythology of ourselves". This wise set of forces, unveils our dreaming selves, and so much more, at night, while we're asleep and also in waking visionary states. Working with the energies that are revealed in these spaces appears to be one of the most reliable forms of relating with authentic and intelligent powers that are other than waking physical, known realities. Such labor tends to evoke our deep, cultured and primordial selves while also describing and outlining our own and nature's observable limits. Such engagements with the imagination also put us in contact with the other forms of life with which we share the earth and the spirit planes. In dreams, we engage with plants, animals, elements, spirits and other people, to begin with.

PROJECTION

Due to the limiting nature of what is known - and of what is not known or is being remembered - we humans *project*.

A really simple way to begin to understand projection is to note that we each see and experience things in ways that are unique and shared, both. Two people see an eagle. Both see the eagle as an eagle, with its winged feathers and alert eyes hovering above its beak. For one, however, the eagle evokes feelings, images and ideas of great freedom and power, thoughts about what it means to live within the cradle of the Holy Divine in Nature. The other, at the same time, recalls once having witnessed an eagle in the forest as it fed itself from another, smaller bird's nest on freshly hatched eggs. One person sees a kind of beauty and the other a kind of destructiveness. Who's right? From a broad view, the answer is *both*. What each person sees in the eagle describes some aspect of its' being, and also, very likely, aspects of the people doing the seeing.

A key reason for augmenting our perception of projection, is to be able to recognize that we each see and experience vital layers of existence that are possible to mutually recognize. At the same time we also each see different aspects of the same jewel that appear unique for a variety of reasons. To a large extent, what we see depends on our individual, yet shared angles of perspective and prior learning. What do we see that is universally, even naturally ordered, and what portion belongs to our own private backgrounds? How do these contributing factors relate to our modes of discerning reality for ourselves and in communities?

I have to admit that I don't much like the word "projection". It feels somehow overly abstract and evokes a more scientific bent. At the same time, I haven't yet found another exact way of referring to this important phenomenon. When we seek to know what we place outside ourselves, that may be out there, but also arises from within, it's as though we're becoming involved in a vital creative project for our own and others lives and well-being. Making distinctions around these projects addresses some of the most troubling and divisive tendencies we craft together as people.

Projections, or the projects of our lives, influence how we ethically relate to one another and the world. Marie-Louise von Franz has written an entire book about this, called *Projection and Re-collection, Reflections of the Soul*. In this guiding work, she defines projection right off the bat in the following way, referring to Jung's rendering of the phenomenon behind projection,

> " He (Jung) used the word to describe a psychological fact that can be observed everywhere in the everyday life of human beings, namely, that in our ideas about other people and situations we are often liable to make certain

misjudgments that we are likely to have to correct, having acquired better insight."[5]

To become aware of projection is to seek to know the ocean of experience and meaning within and without, to know that these waters contain much more than the eye can see. Knowledge, experience, belonging and meaning are alive within us, the world and the universe, but we're not fully aware of these. When we engage our ability to articulate what is within and beyond us, we may then realize that we can be somewhat conscious of and can look at what is unknown or forgotten. We can feel it, sense it, describe it, acknowledging and fashioning existence from these raw materials.

Here are some examples, to ground this theoretical musing a bit. In human relationships, we witness the way the projects of our lives influence our undertakings. A man who grew up with an extremely protective mother is likely to see these qualities present in certain women that he relates to when they are seeking to offer support to him. Many women will tend to see their fathers in other men as well. A lot of women have experienced what we call "the absent father". When a man in such a woman's life shows any signs of independence, she is likely to experience feelings of what we call abandonment. The past has a tendency to create inner constructs, which we carry forward into the present, whether they still apply or not.

Rattled war veterans coming home from the battlefield will often go into warrior mode when confronted with any noise that remotely resembles traumatizing events beheld during their time of service. I once had a client tell me not to stand behind him. I asked why and he said that he still hadn't gotten over a self-defensive tendency he had developed while in prison. He explained how he learned to attack or be atacked under such circumstances during his lock-up days. My client told me that, despite recognizing that he was no longer in prison, he couldn't stop himself from acting that out in the present.

Even when we talk about the weather, we project. A winter storm blows through town and folks use words like "nasty" and "brutal" to describe the effects of the elements upon everyday life. However, the wind, rain, snow and cold aren't necessarily acting badly – that's a human value and, hence, a form of projection.

In all these instances, what's occurring is that individuals are casting their former memories, feelings and learning out onto present circumstances as a result of previous experiences or internal value judgments. In these moments, the reality taking place outside will tend to resemble the past to a certain degree.

A definite form of projection is the way we find qualities in others that we don't want to admit about ourselves, which we find difficult to accept. In our culture here in the West, many tend to want to deny disharmony. So we see these characteristics in others, like people from cultures in foreign countries, and single them out as flawed or even evil. This isn't to say that these elements aren't present when we note them outside in others. We say in this work, "just because it's a projection doesn't mean that it isn't true". At the same time, what bothers us about others is often something that we find troubling about ourselves. Throughout the course of human history, those who are different or set apart have been labeled as wrong and mistaken.

We project ideas, meanings and feelings onto people, phenomena and events outside ourselves all the time. Primarily, we project so that we can understand and learn from our experience, and become aware of what we weren't previously in the direct speech-ripe presence of. On an important level, it's not as if projecting is inherently a bad thing. Because there is always going to be a limit to what we know on a conscious, waking level, we actually need our projections so that we can realize seemingly hidden truths of being that exist inside and outside our selves as well. At any given time, we cast outside ourselves what we think or feel is happening, so that we can engage with and understand the world, our selves and each other. What we do with these projects makes all the difference, in the long run.

We can access and relate to the realities within and without by working with our dreams. We project based on what we've learned, and also based on deep inner memories and eternally unfolding patterns of being, formed in the crucibles and rivers of the soul's mighty flowing energies and the Spirit World's heaving oceans of vital essence.

It's not as though everything comes from within us. Truths and realities exist independent of projection, of course. Yet, we might come to see that all these energies connect on very important levels of being.

I AM THAT TOO, "PROJECT INTERCONNECTION"

It's a lot like the fact that even though we're moving about in these wondrous bodies, most of the time we're barely even aware that there is an enormous amount of activity taking place below the surface of our skin.

Von Franz again,

"Just as we cannot 'see' into the depths of the waters, so the deeper areas of the unconscious are also invisible to us."[6]

Turn your attention to your own body now, and note the way that you can choose to seek to be aware of what's taking place. Can you simultaneously know what is occurring in, around and upon your physique, all at the same time? When turning our attention to what's taking place, it seems we can only be sure of paying attention to a few activities, like breathing, the sun and wind on the skins and maybe the heartbeat in the chest. Beyond this, even though I can seek to observe my pulse or the great alchemy of my innards, I still only sense part of what's going on there. I don't see the tissues or the movement, the pumping of blood, or the vibrancy that's happening inside and on minute levels. I can look at my outer form, my skin, my chest, my legs and arms. At the same time I hardly have any awareness - and how many of us do? - of my backside. What's going on back there and deep within? If this is the case with our own bodies, how much more so with the cornucopia of existence that can be found in the world, not to mention in the Dreaming!

So it is with the inner world of the psyche. Just as there are apparent physical laws, which relate to physical matter, there are observable qualities of consistent characteristics in the domains of the soul, the "wilderness of our selves".

In various spiritual traditions, projection has been well described for many long years. Christianity speaks of it in scripture where the injunction arises to take the beam out of one's own eye rather than pointing to the splinter in another's. Hindus have the Sanskrit saying *Tat Tvam Asi*, meaning, "I am that too". This phrase demonstrates a sophisticated understanding of interconnection by acknowledging the felt and observed fact that when we look at someone outside ourselves, it's wise to reflect on how what we witness also exists within. I'm also quite fond of the old Mayan saying *Inlakesh*, which I understand is a way of acknowledging how, "I am the other you". These are modes of deep understanding and speaking that can honor how, on a certain level – one richly demonstrated in the practice of sharing and remembering dreams together – *all is interwoven, connected and related while also diverse.*

Because there is much that we have yet to learn and know, I believe we would do best to assume an attitude of curiosity towards attempts at living our lives amid the warp and weave of the world and alongside the many creatures with whom we share the journey. I have a canny hunch, based on my own and others experience, that there will *always* be more to learn. When what we seem to know doesn't work or fit, or when we're overly certain that we know what's right or true in a given situation, we might step back and ask ourselves if perhaps something unconscious in us or in our experience is seeking to become known. It's entirely likely that greater wisdom and understanding are seeking to come to the fore in the surprising fields of our experience.

One of the best ways I have found to honor that there is much that we don't already know is to listen to the dreams, viewpoints and ideas that we receive and hold, and to those near to us. Sometimes even ideas and opinions belonging to people who seem to be the most set apart from how we see ourselves can reveal the most about them and us. We can't know what we don't know until it appears, and even then, we are likely to label it as some approximation of what is already familiar, rather than what it truly is. If we can cultivate a taste for being with the unknown, we can allow ourselves to admit the possibility that what looks like one thing may be entirely different than we thought it was or ought to be.

Again, an example may help us come into a relatable storied experience. A dreamer in one of my regular ongoing groups shared a dream featuring Michelle and Barrack Obama doing a dream world drive-by. The dreamer stated how, in the dream, the presidential pair appear behind her while she reaches out and gives the President a high five. Michelle is at the driver's wheel.

While imagining this dream for ourselves, several of us in the dream group felt that this was the dreaming source's way of suggesting that the dreamer herself could be reclaiming some personal power that had previously been left behind. The woman who shared the dream stated being fairly befuddled about why these two would come to her during the night. Yet the recalled experience showed a willingness to reach out and make contact with these powerful and highly culturally imagined individuals.

Obama and his wife are truly what we call public personas. I very much doubt that the rest of us know anything significant in the way of truly personal information about this couple. In other words, *they carry our projections* of who and what the First Lady and the President are supposed to be and represent, in addition to all the extra ideas we will inevitably have about the first African American presidential pair. Therefore, their appearance in the dream evokes various qualities in each of us, as we see and feel them when we imagine that we're the ones reaching out to make contact with "The Prez", and as we imagine ourselves as Barrack and Michelle.

The dreamer of this dreamscape who shared the dream agreed with the group's projected insights. It seemed that there was something here about "behind every great man there is a great woman". This hunch seemed to suggest the dreamer's own call to embodied empowerment in her life, as well as in the group participants lives, when we held our versions of the dream in mind and at heart. This resonant situation in the dream evoked a helpful message for each of us about outwardly placed projections onto the Obamas. The dream seemed to be saying, 'nudge' 'nudge', these are the leading energies inherent in our own lives and souls, dressed up to look like the leaders of the western world!

Through dreams, the aspects of our being that we have yet to become fully aware of in waking life show up in our psyches. It is truly as if some greater, heartful intelligence is feeding us wisdom via the dream world. This great, often terrifying, creative-destructive, helpful-troublesome and sometimes, also dangerous presence appears to have an investment in the wholeness of all living beings. To a large extent, this is a mystery, yet one that we can apprentice ourselves to from the standpoint of being interested in learning, loving, living and dying well, while also practicing a healthy dose of skepticism so that we don't simply accept what is being offered without some amount of discernment. Honest and repeated work with dreams reveals a wealth of understandable, pragmatic information and experience, which rounds out our ability to live full lives and approach our deaths with honesty and intelligence.

We may seek to ally ourselves with these energies in the effort of becoming more conscious and creative. That is to say, more knowledgeable, imaginative and aware. As we do so, we notice that each time we place our attention in one direction, the tendency to lose the focus on another area seems to be inherent in the practice. We can talk of "becoming conscious". And yet, it seems wise to consider that there will always be more to learn, know and understand. Who amongst us can truly demonstrate the ability to be aware of all that is, all the time?

MANY PAIRS OF EYES, WORKING IN GROUPS

Work with dreams in groups can help us see what we don't already know or may have forgotten and offers enormous benefits. Often, we come to a more diverse and ever-unfolding understanding of the many levels displayed in the dreams as we are assisted to see for ourselves what we find difficult to acknowledge in our uniquely limited perspectives. By courageously sharing our dreams with one another, we are also serving a greater practice of keeping a steady lookout for the elements within individual and shared experience that we tend to miss when we reflect in isolation. It's like the old saying, "Two pairs of eyes are better than one".

> Jeremy Taylor describes some rewards of group work, "Because all dreams have multiple layers of significance, the chances of a dreamer actually reaching something approaching the full range of meanings in any given dream are much greater working with the multiple suggestions and projections of a group than working in solitude..."[7]

Naturally, it's helpful to seek to understand our dreams for ourselves, by ourselves, and some amount of revelation will always happen in this pursuit also. And yet, when we work alone, it's as if we're trying to see what lies behind us while staring firmly ahead.

If I was by myself and wanted to see my own backside, I'd have to use at least two mirrors to do so. What I'd see would be distorted somehow through the act of looking in these reflections at slightly removed angles. This adds up to a lot of work that I don't have to do alone. What if I had someone I could trust look at my back and tell me what lies there? I'd get the report a lot more quickly, though I'd want to be sure that I account for the fact that, the person telling me about my rear would also be reporting through their own unique filters of interpretation.

There's an inherent paradox in this. In order to unravel what's real for oneself, we need to draw upon the support of others. Group work, or one to one inquiry, is also dependent on the clear understanding that others can tell us what they see, but only we can be sure for ourselves what is true as it pertains to our own lives. At the same time, there will always be essentials that make themselves known as relatives to the transpersonal domain of our mutual human ken. In other words, there is the personal and also the collective, the private and the shared. These truly do overlap.

In my years of facilitating group work with diverse collections of dreamers, I've witnessed how helpful it is for a full spectrum of varying ideas to be projected onto the dreams. People who share dreams in groups, myself included, almost always say that they have been able to see things about the dreams and their meanings that they weren't aware of when looking on their own.

The way I state this in a simple guideline is as follows, "The dreamer is the only person who can ultimately verify the meaning and validity of dreams and their messages." (Wernet)

The ultimate authority on the meaning of any dream is the dreamer. Myself and many other dreamers and dream workers have found this to be a crucial and rewarding standpoint and one that respects the dreamer and his or her choices about how to view, act upon and understand the dreams, as well as how to choose to work with their energies of vital guidance.

With this understanding in place around dream work, we may also witness that all insights about any dream will necessarily be an outgrowth of projection. When folks are new to this work, I encourage them to entertain the idea that this is the case, and then to see if it appears to be true. The way this looks is, people agree to use "I language" such as, "when I imagine this dream for myself, it seems to be saying to me that in my life and dream…" This ingenious style allows one and all to find meaning in the dreams.

We are so used to speaking from a removed position, by saying things like, "when you want to make a change in your life, you have to…!" Often, we attempt to find common ground through our communication by invoking what we could call "You language". This manner of speaking seems to me like an attempt to demonstrate universal understanding, at its best. It also tends to create hostile levels of protective defensiveness and to demonstrate efforts at control, at its worst. What seems more helpful, at least in exploring our dreams together, if not in almost all situations in our lives, is to own that the way we see, feel and think about things is actually how "I" see it and to adjust our language. At times we may agree and others disagree. This is how we learn about new possibilities and viewpoints.

Such a practice has the benefit of encouraging us to take responsibility for our own lives. We then get to reflect upon how we see things based on how others experience them, in addition to how we perceive life to be from our own unique yet equally shared, human positions.

Working with dreams in this way simply honors the truth of what is actually happening. When one person in a group shares a dream, and the rest listen, we all experience, create, or *dream-up* our own version of the remembered advent. Some aspects of the

dream and what is heard will be imagined as clearly universal –
understood and shared by each person in the group. Just like with
the earlier example of the two people who see an eagle, if I reveal
a dream with a snake in it, everyone who's receiving the dream
will have some notion of what a snake is which all people present
would agree upon. At the same time, most, if not all folks, have
had different experiences of snakes. Some people have touched a
snake, or may have even been bitten by one, and still others may
have only seen a snake in pictures, movies, paintings or dreams.
Throughout time, snakes have held certain levels of symbolic and
transpersonal, archetypal meanings for people too. On one
important level, the snake is also what it is, no matter individual
notions of it. So, to speak about the snake as we each see it, know
it, imagine it and understand it is really just an honoring of how
things really are to a great extent. We each have our own version
of the dream snake in addition to a collective resonance with it.
Both and more are crucial to our being able to learn from and
relate to snakes, to each other and to waking life in general.

Equally true is the fact that, whatever ideas anyone has
about what the snake might represent or mean, no matter where
these ideas have been picked up or learned, such notions may or
may not apply to the dream and the dreamer. Therefore, it's always
more helpful to allow the dreamer to decide for herself or himself

if the associations or ideas of other dreamers in a group strike a chord. And so it is, also, in the events of everyday life.

We've covered some "heady" ground in this chapter. Perhaps it will serve to look to the poignancy of the poetic to further unfurl these many ideas. Dreams involve the myriad faculties of our beings. The spirit and soul of *poesis* can provide a honey jar for the knowledge and experience to be found in our imaginative, vital, unfolding lives. Rumi speaks to the nature of knowing and not knowing in his poem, *Looking Into the Creek* from Coleman Barks' rendition in *The Soul of Rumi,*

> "The way the soul is with the senses and the intellect is like a creek. When desire weeds grow thick, intelligence can't flow, and the soul creatures stay hidden.
> But sometimes the reasonable clarity runs so strong it sweeps the clogged stream open. No longer weeping and frustrated, your being grows as powerful as your wantings were before, more so. Laughing and satisfied, the masterful flow lets creations of the soul appear. You look down, and it's lucid dreaming. The gates made of light swing open. You see in."[8]

Endnotes Chapter 1

[1] Carl Jung, "The Jung Reader", David Tacey, Routledge, 2012, p. 65

[2] Jeremy Taylor, "The Living Labyrinth", Paulist Press, New York, 1998, p. 263

[3] Martin Shaw, "A Branch From the Lightning Tree", White Cloud Press, Ashland Oregon, 2011, p.117

[4] Jeremy Taylor, "The Living Labyrinth", Paulist Press, New York, 1998, p.11

[5] Marie-Louise von Franz, "Projection and Re-Collection in Jungian Psychology, Reflections of the Soul", Open Court, Chicago and La Salle, 1995, p. 1

[6] Marie-Louise von Franz, "Projection and Re-Collection in Jungian Psychology, Reflections of the Soul", Open Court, Chicago and La Salle, 1995, p. 185

[7] Jeremy Taylor, "The Wisdom of Your Dreams", Tarcher-Penguin, New York New York, 2009, p. 117

[i8] Coleman Barks, "The Soul of Rumi", HarperCollins, New York, 2002, p. 38

CHAPTER 2

Apocalypse Again, the Many Layers of Healing in Dreams

"There'll be a breaking of the ancient western code, your private life will suddenly explode, there'll be phantoms and fires on the road..."
Leonard Cohen, "The Future"

The mere experience of any dream itself is healing.

Practicing group or individual work, dream experiences are recalled and reach a greater level of awareness, inviting us to integrate their fabrics of soul that show up in myriad ways. In simply holding a willingness to witness the dreams and our memories of them while awake, we are bringing these experiences towards deepened intelligence.

Consider one of the basic understandings of Projective-style Dream Work, that there are no truly "bad dreams". In seeking to understand the way we form unhelpful standpoints in relation to the more challenging layers of our existence, time and again, the dreamer who shares a dream has the felt-sense that what looked awful at first, is actually an important message full of vital healing gifts to bestow. I've seen this happen over and over in dreaming communities.

Myself, and many others who have worked with dreams *know* that *dreams and dream work are profoundly healing*. We know this from first-hand felt experiences of the personal, collectively shared transformations that regularly arise out of the rivers of our dreams. Cultures around the world and through time have known for thousands of years that dreams heal and bear practical reflections about how to live and die.

The capacity for healing through dreams, art, story and music is quintessentially important and wildly enriching. Artful disciplines and energies of the Imagination provide what we could call a 'full color' approach to a fulsome sense of belonging and of wholeness.

THE NATURE OF OUR NATURE NATURING

The word "healing" itself bears a close relationship to the word "wholeness". In *The Dictionary of Word Origins*, under the entry for the word "health", we find the following,

"Etymologically, *health* is the 'state of being whole…'"[1]

Wholeness and healing are close relatives of what has been called the Holy. Wholeness embodies a felt-sense of totality. To heal is to become whole, to come into right relation with the very nature of existence and belonging on many levels. To experience our nature is to be connected to and feel a lifeline to Great Nature itself, or as I like to speak of it, *the nature of Nature naturing*. Wholeness means pain and joy, suffering and pleasure, grief and love, as well as all the in betweens and beyonds related to these. As the old alchemists say, wholeness is alike to "a warring peace, a sweet wound, an agreeable evil".

Dreams bid us to engage wholeness every night as we sleep. The obstacles we have inherited, encountered or avoided during daylight hours and via threads of the soul show up on our doorstep while we're in a physical and psychological, spiritual state of surrender. What we have overlooked, forgotten, tried to hide from, or are simply about the task of remembering, returns, seemingly uninvited, while we're bathed in the darkness of night, vulnerable in our beds.

The blackened mare of the night rides us and takes us on rowdy journeys where we become party to unexpected visions and heart-pounding adventures. In our dreams we come face to face with energies that don't seem to originate at all from our usual sense of the waking world. We partake of situations while dreaming that suggest the missing pieces of the puzzle that we're seeking to complete in our daily lives while we're asleep. Dreams connect us to the eternal, as well as the timely. The trouble is, we have a hard time seeing that this is so from our habitual waking viewpoints. In our dreaming we are met by forces that we could call foreign to our daytime awareness.

Dreamers, poets, storytellers, musicians and artists have known for ages that vital energies of existence enflesh themselves in the multi-faceted wonders we call *metaphors*. From a soul work view, metaphors aren't stand-ins. These beings, who carry across, back and forth, *are what they are and more*. They simply do not inhabit the kind of material reality we have grown accustomed to defining as "real".

Martin Shaw, storyteller and unruly, wise apple poacher, helps craft an alive understanding towards this,

> "Metaphor is the great leap, the generous offering of many possibilities contained in one image… the poetic is not attempting to offer proof but representation."[2]

That which metaphor *re-presents* is best stood beneath, understood, in a compressed-yet-expansive manner. Think of a multi-faceted jewel and all the many views and angles it comprises, and you'll get the drift. Imagine seeing the view from within the jewel. How many divergent visions do you behold there? This is an energetic reality that lives in the very leaping itself. By inhabiting this genius and condensed yet enlarging space of many possibilities, dreams, stories, music, poems, art, any discipline that reveals metaphor to our awareness, all seek to give us as much as they might. It's a matter of exasperating and breath-filled kinds of creative economy. The profound tapestry of dreams and imagination are woven through the leaping to be found within metaphors and symbols.

Symbols themselves aren't mere signs. They don't simply refer to something else, like a pointing finger, any more than metaphors do. They are *larger-than-ordinary-life* beings reflecting an innumerable creativity of elements. These forces take the form they do so that spontaneity can be witnessed in the many corners of the castle of the mind, upon the altars of the heart and throughout the forests of the body. The word *symbol* itself means, "thrown together". Symbolic reality, like metaphorical essence and being, *is* what it *is*. Carl Jung's work focuses on recognizing the way symbols come to us to embody our relationship with what is reasonable, and also to refer to what we could name as irrational.

Marie-Louise von Franz writes,
"A symbol is an image that *expresses an essential…* unknown, indeed to something that is never *quite*

knowable... It is... made visible through the fact that it activates and groups the material available for representation... the archetype, in itself unknowable, clothes itself, so to speak, in this material..."[3]

Sit with and gaze upon the symbol of a spiral. Only a spiral can do exactly what it does. It evokes the energy of a center radiating out in ever-expanding kindred circles, leading to a real sense of the temporal and an embodiment of the never-ending. Dreams, stories, art and songs are composed of such living "essential" materials. As they can deliver us to these beings or ferry them over to us, we experience glittering versatile treasure troves of meaning and being that we could, perhaps, relate to in no better way.

How do dreams heal? Metaphors and symbols live in the world, our psyches and in the body. Marion Woodman, another well-known Jungian whose work is steeped in the creative arts, tells us they are imaged instincts. From one view, each of us has a sacred tree winding up our middles. There's a holy snake winding through its branches, whose form is also hugging the trunk, its tail resting up at base camp. The leaf-filled nests up top are awash with birdsong, the many ideas, inspirations and thoughts that land and sprout in those branches, and the roots twine down through our legs and feet to help us maintain our living connection with the ground beneath us. The trunk houses the true jewels of the heart and from time to time invites, gives and receives a wonderfully enclosing embrace. All these energies and forms inter-relate. This small vision is like a view from inside the storied dream of the body.

In our severely demythologized culture of material literalism and reasonable livelihoods, we have forgotten such simple yet cannily profound truths as these. *Remembering the whole heals*. We are, each of us, merely one weave of the many fabrics of the expansive garment of belonging. Dreams remind us that we are also nature, *naturing* in a great dance whose rhythm is designed for the regaining of deep memory and purpose amid the very human crafting of culture as a blood-woven relative and integral force of the Cosmos and the Holy Divine in Nature.

GREAT FORGETTINGS, HOLY REMEMBRANCES

Storytelling traditions uphold that we human beings are the great amnesiacs. We are time and again pulled into visions that seek to remind us that this is so. It's as if we become fooled by life into forgetting the deep relations we bear within the wholes of existence.

Stories, dreams and artful renderings that speak to this can be found in cultures and people's lives around the world. In one way or another, in each tale that relays the inevitability of such forgetting, the true sense of the sacred and a sacred sense of truth are lost and then found. The regaining of such memory can only be had after the following through and suffering of certain trials.

It's like the old East Indian tale about Sudama, a common village youth and Krishna, Divine Lord of Ecstasy. This seemingly inseparable pair gamboled around together as children. Yet they eventually went different directions through the unavoidable travails of earthly life and the revelation of the Goatherd's godly identity. In their younger days and nights, they made music together, ate sweets, laughed, adventured and dreamt the way young people do. For Sudama, these were some of the richest times he had ever known.

When a monster serpent arose out of the river near the center of the village one day, Krishna unpredictably wrestled it into submission. With his sacred nature thus uncloaked, he and his family departed to a far off palace, away from the common locale of their humble origins, and also from Sudama and his kin.

Forlorn yet fated to remain, Sudama grew into his life as a simple village man. He partook of the daily round that this required. He married, had children and worked. The days went by, full of mundane drudgery. Faint, sorrowful yet sweet memories of his glorious youth beside Krishna kept him awake on many nights. He eventually became so troubled he was practically unable to focus on the tasks at hand. So it was that his wise wife, Padmini, eventually suggested he go and seek out Krishna for the recalling of the beauty and wonder that their playful and innocent connection betokened in them, so long ago.

Doubting that Krishna would even recognize him, feeling purposeless and alone, Sudama eventually agreed to set off and seek his old friend out. Along the way he stopped for a nap and beheld a dream in which he was once again together with his great friend. The dream seemed so real and simple and Sudama was overjoyed to be close to Krishna once more. Upon awakening he made the same mistake so many of us do by bemoaning the apparent fact that, "it was only a dream". He almost turned around and went home at the last minute. After much hemming and hawing, he decided that he had to go all the way, to at least see his long journey through. It was as though the dream was pulling him towards something Sudama couldn't see, as yet.

Well, you may know how these things go, or you may not, but soon you will, one way or another. Sudama arrived by the gates of the magnificent and otherworldly palace. So many amazing sights and sounds did he behold there! Ambrosia wafted on the gentle winds, sensuous and delicious strains of melody reached out and plucked at his heart strings, and more colors than the eye could properly behold rushed down like a mighty waterfall upon him. The musicians present were of such a caliber of mystical appeal and mastery that he murmured to himself how Krishna would surely not have any interest whatsoever in his own outworn and earthy, threadbare musings.

Soon thereafter, as if up from out of the deep core of this resplendent scene, Krishna appeared. Sudama announced himself saying, "You probably don't remember me..." The Divine One interrupted and countered his old friend, saying that of course he remembered him and was overjoyed to find him there! The two grew close once more, playing music and revisiting the joyful abandon of their youths, yet now as full grown men.

Sudama stayed with Krishna for quite some time. Who knows how long a time it was? Some say days or months and others, years. After this indefinite period, Sudama was in due course given to realizing that he had always been welcome in the court of his friend, Lord Krishna. He understood and felt himself to be a brother to the Great Cowherd and a necessary voice for the unique form of the sacred that only he could bring in the close-to-earth way that he did. At last, however, he also understood that his place was beside his wife and that his children needed him to return and share the blessings that came from dwelling in Krishna's company.

So, although it pained him and also brought some joy to leave, he journeyed homewards and invited his loving partner Padmini to join him in the woods in a hut he had found along the way. In this place, Sudama sensed they could fashion a life and a death together, honoring all that had come before, and might follow afterwards. She agreed to his behest and the two acknowledged that their children were of age to take up the family inheritance in the world of the village. They bequeathed their small estate to them and headed off.

The couple thus made their home in the little wayside enclosure in the wilderness, halfway between their old village and Krishna's palace at Vrindavana where they drummed, sang and played music, along with the birds and beasts of the wood, in a genuine devotion to the Holy Divine throughout the remaining days and nights of their human lives.

This tale reveals, to any who would listen, threads of sacred recollection around the all-too-human experience of dealing with the ordinary tasks of everyday life. It also speaks to the tasks of becoming an adult, and potentially, a kind of elder. In the dawning awareness of Krishna's divinity, alongside Sudama's keenly felt humanity, we get a taste of the tendency to forget to take up and live out our own sacred inheritance. We could reflect upon how we also struggle to feel worthy for the realization that we are woven into and by the Divine. This has to do with our forgetting, like Sudama, the way we are deeply related to the spiritual as well as the physical. This amnesia is a natural consequence of our need to make a way in the humbling, complicated human villages we live amongst in the waking world. We think we are somehow separate until we gather the courage to remember, that is to say, put back together again, the kingly and queenly qualities in our own souls.

Similarly, on the opposite end of the spectrum, we note the subduing of the water dragon early on by Krishna. This defining event reveals his godly nature. It also bespeaks a kind of grandiosity, its troubling tendency to come as a surprise and seek to swallow the whole village up if it can. Where the Sudama we also are feels unworthy, others may surmise an over-worthiness that assumes monstrous proportions. The story seems to say, the Divine will not allow this inflated energy to consume the village. The sacred itself is a grandiose force, and once identified, becomes located apart from yet somehow also remains connected to everyday affairs. We see this play out in the story where Krishna and his family move off to Vrindivana. The people know where to find Krishna, no less. On one level, it's a case of recognizing the holy as part of earthly life. On another, it's also about paradoxically acknowledging that, even though humans and divinities can and do relate and even may live together at times, the Divine is a power to be reckoned with. The human is necessarily also human. Why else would we be here playing this grief-laden and ecstatic game of forgetting and remembering in these skin-enclosed star-shaped bags of flesh and bones?

This motif of losing track, and then recalling again these deep truths appears in myths, dreams and folk traditions to remind us of something vital to belonging. We'd do well to distinguish that there is some central knowledge to be found in this tendency to forget. With hard work, good fortune and the help of others, we may also craft ways of remembering and being recalled.

THE MEMORY KEEPERS OF THE NIGHT

Similarly to Sudama, as we sleep and dream we encounter something imperative about our own true natures and are invited to make the journey of waking with remembrance. We tend to overlook or simply neglect what takes place in the dreaming. And yet, we may still seek to regain that sense of deeper identity and co-relation through creative disciplines. The very fact that our dreams seek us out says that some needed recollection is trying to make itself known, if only we will dare to listen.

To give a grounded example of this as it appears in dreams, consider that men and women in modern societies, at different times in their lives, dream about lost, missing or stolen driver's licenses, purses and passports. This occurrence in dreams is quite similar to forgetting who one is. It's a species of questioning where a valid form of identity might actually arise. Is identity socially defined, a geographical given, how much one owns or does not own or possibly one's physical appearance? Perhaps it includes, yet is far more than any of these.

This is the dreaming source's way of showing we're not just who we think we are while we're awake. Missing I.D. papers and wallets in dreams suggest that we are more than our cultivated ideas and identities. Beyond what our societal roles are, we are also animals, wild forces of nature. We are souls and spirits too, defined by what and how we are, more than what we're called or where we live or our given job title in the world. At the same time, we are all of these things, and importantly so. Some cultures base a person's identity primarily on one's relationship to the surrounding land, elements, plants and creatures that inhabit and characterize a well cared for "dreaming of place".

One of the major tasks of dreams, I'm convinced, is to show that we are not only formed human personalities or egos. We are also relatives of the Sacred, in earthly and otherworldly forms.

Do we live like we are? To forget who we seem to be 'officially' in our dreams forms a recollection into an open, grounded and true sense of shared, primal, spiritual and soul identity.

Another way this shows up is in dreams of encounters with forces that appear *larger-than-life*. Dreams of towering mountains, massive foam-laden ocean waves, shining mounds of glistening gold, to name a few symbolic dream personages, could all indicate larger than human identities seeking us out while dreaming. We could again recall the river monster that Krishna and Sudama met in our tale. These elements show up around the world and throughout time in folk-myths and fairy tales, as well as in dreams, as living, human and non-human personalities, evoking aspects of life and death, within and without.

Often, dream-threads of conflict are the personal and collective mythic motifs that arise. When they do, the ego can tend to feel threatened by the enormity of the call to a bigger sense of identity as proposed by the Dreaming. The ego that appears as the "me" that I seem to be in the dreams (and in waking life) often finds itself in struggles that clearly represent the tension that is felt between a known and secure idea of identity and a more limitless and unfamiliar wellspring. It's not uncommon for apparently invasive and threatening occurrences to take place in the dream-space, symbolizing the ego's experience of being faced by Spirit, or the Divine.

Even "natural disasters" such as tidal waves, hurricanes or tornadoes symbolize and evoke this meeting between what we can call the small self and the Big Self. Such dreams tend to comment on waking life circumstances of the past and the future. Yet they also always speak in symbols and metaphors that replenish much wider kinds of understandings about our place within this waking world, and also in the spirit realms *in the present*.

THE SWAMPLANDS OF THE SOUL

Let's look at a storied advent that illustrates all of this and more. This is the dream of a woman who attends one of my on-going community dream groups.

"Sheena the Destroyer"

At first there are two women - myself and another. It feels post-apocalyptic. We are in a swamp area. Twisted, snake-like trees surround us and shield the view of the sky for the most part. I get the feeling that there are mountains surrounding us and we are in the valley. Everyone is in pain or has died. There are boardwalks extending out of the swampy water, which is nearby. There's dancing, movement and music. The beat is enchanting, sultry and eerie at the same time.

As I'm dancing, I notice my physical body is part tree and my bark is paper thin and bloody. As I notice myself in this way, I become aware of fear. My clothes are hanging off, tattered & torn, ripped and shredded. Blackened places appear on my skin as if I've been through a fire. I realize the other woman who is with me is a close and dear friend from waking life; we're searching for her parents. I think to myself, "She's going to be upset that they're dead."

She and I are trying to protect each other and look for resources out of 'what's left' after the apocalypse. There are fragments of a house that's still standing around us. I see there are holes in the roof and walls, and yet, places where one can go to feel at home, to shelter and hide from what's happened. I'm looking for other survivors, and realize I feel frightened of what will come up out of the water.

I also feel sadness and loss as I look around at the wreckage. I then get a sense of a strong third female presence and a woman rises up out of the swamp. Her body is part tree like mine, but she is large, tall, strong and powerful. I know she represents darkness. I wake up with the sense of being tickled under both arms and am then jolted awake.

Upon awakening, the dreamer felt moved to dialogue with Sheena, the third woman who appears at the end of the dream. The following is the dream-like report of that interaction.

Dreamer, *"Who are you?"*

Dream Woman, *"I am Sheena the Destroyer."*

Dreamer, *"Why have you come?"*

Sheena, *"I want you to see your own destructive behavior. You all (humankind) fall away and disintegrate into nothing. You are not immune to death, sickness, disease and violence. All is a part of your path of life. You cannot pretend otherwise. I want you to see that your health is important. You can choose to live here and ignore it, but you will always be connected and a part of it. You can choose to embrace me and I will be your friend.*

Dreamer, *"How?"*

Sheena, *"Do your cleanse, get back to the pure light within you.*

After this dialogue, the dreamer feels intuitively moved to take an imaginal sword as part of her semi-waking, semi-asleep vision and chops Sheena into little pieces. This mighty divine woman then floats back into the swamp and the dreamer knows she will grow back again into new life.

This dream, like all dreams, has come to the dreamer and others who imagine it for themselves, to uncover a bevy of wholeness-inducing messages of meaning and experience.

One of the first things to notice is that the setting in the dream-space is one of mayhem in the midst of elements reflecting natural power and wonder. The tone of "post-apocalypse" is a common mythic theme of our age. Referring once more to *the Dictionary of Word Origins,* we may realize that the word apocalypse has only come to mean the literal end of the world over the past one hundred years or so. The original significance of "apocalypse" comes from the Old Latin and Greek and refers to a revelation, from *apokaluptein,* "to uncover and reveal". The above dream contains both the sense of everything coming to an end, and also a revealing of deeper, more primal, inherent, cosmically eternal truths about the beginnings of the end and the endless beginnings seeded within them.

The people in the dream all seem to be women. The dream underscores what many people have been saying for a long time about the way that an imbalanced, power-driven principle in the world and the psyche has had an overall damaging effect for life here on earth. The over-emphasis on masculinist and ascendant, lop-sided standpoints has resulted in the relegation of the sacred feminine into *matter* – a word which, by no accident, means *mother* as well as *into the earth*. I believe this is why the dream features well-known elements that bespeak the energies of Great Goddess mythologies.

Themes of The End have also appeared in similar fashions at prior moments throughout the ages. Apocalypse is an archaic archetype of the unconscious that has surfaced in many narratives, from the South American story of Icanchu's Drum to the more familiar Noah's Ark variety of Christian traditional mythical accounts. In unpacking the dream, we can see how it's true that *all dreams speak on many levels at once and come to tell us things we don't already know, which we may yet remember and learn about.*

On a personal wavelength, the dreamer herself acknowledged strong 'A-ha's of recognition' in connection to the sense of everything being in need of renewal in her own, individual life. The architecture of the dream suggests the energy of what Jung termed "the Original Self" and what I've spoken of above as the larger-than-life energies of the Big Self, contrasted with the more familiar identity of the dream ego, or little self. The latter appears as the dreamer's familiar personality, a tattered woman who is accompanied by another woman whom she knows from waking life. The two are seeking a shelter, the friends' parents and they engage in the very human activity of trying to gather the resources needed for survival in the wake of disaster.

The mountains, trees, swamp and valley create an atmosphere of natural surrounds that echo the reality of *wilderness*. The overall flavor is one of totality, typified by the presence of the heights that are not clearly seen, compared with the lowly swamps, all of which we imagine for ourselves as they appear in the dream. We also see the existence of plants synthesized with animals – the snake-like patterns of the trees and the hint at shared qualities between them and the dreamer. We have water, earth, stone, plants, animals, humans and their constructs, all creatively woven together in the dream. Fire is also present, in the understanding that the dreamer's skin has been blackened through a recent encounter with flames.

The dream evokes the Elements, and therefore, symbolizes a very palpable sense of wholeness. Jungian dream interpretation is based, in large part, on the idea of *compensation*. This is the notion that the dreams will always point out what is missing from the waking viewpoint of the dreamer, and also in the collective's awareness. Seen from this angle, we again note that the dream is heavy on feminine energy – it doesn't directly feature any masculine character in human form near as we can tell. This tips us off that, even though hints of wholeness are present in the dream, there may also be an observable way in which an imbalance is being depicted. If the wholeness in the dream were complete, we'd expect to find masculine as well as feminine people and energy.

Hence, we see the dream revealing what's likely to be out of balance. By comparing this with what appears to be the case in waking life, we can determine how the dream makes light of what is missing from the conscious view. We can also discover what may be appearing in consciousness as overly one-sided. In the daylit reality of western civilization, we can see that masculine principles tend to far outweigh the energies of their corresponding feminine counterparts. One need only reflect that the vast majority of political and power positions in social life have been filled by men for hundreds upon hundreds of years to see how this is the case.

Houses in dreams often reflect the position of the personality. After all, houses are where humans in the modern era will likely feel most secure. Consider Jeremy Taylor's words on dream houses from his dream symbols book accompanied by the soulful photography of Diane Farris, titled, *Dream Images*,

> "The house is a primary symbol for the self. All imagery and experience in a dream is self-reflective, and the house tends to be particularly reflective of the individual dreamer."[4]

In dreams we can also locate the presence of what Jung called the Self ("Seele" in German, meaning *Soul*). This is the Deep Self, as contrasted with the small self. Sheena, who comes forth later in the dream-story, equally looks to be a potent embodiment of the Soul or Big Self.

Marie-Louise von Franz tells us in her *Interpretation of Fairy Tales,* it's not enough to simply say that the Self appears in the dream or story. What is specific to this actual appearance that can tell us more about what the dream is seeking to communicate *about* the Self? The Self, as elaborated upon in Jungian psychology, is an embodiment of the divine in the psyche. This energy may be aligned with, by the ego, as an orienting center that serves a purpose ruled by principles of connection between the individual *and the collective, which serves and unites both* while also maintaining a healthy regard for diversity, limits and differences. This force of the Self would also seem to exist apart from human beings as its own mysterious yet knowable entity.

In this dream, the house has been partially knocked down, and battered – it has holes in it. There are still places one can go to seek refuge and shelter "to hide from what's happened". There's a sense here that such an experience has to do with a tendency to want to find safety and comfort in the face of the enormous changes that are brought about by apocalyptic –uncovering, revealing - energies. This is an ego confrontation with the greatness of inner and outer life that is seeking to make known a deeper set of truths for the care-taking of the individual and "the Other", for nature and for human culture-making. Here is a coming to terms with the tearing down of the old built-up forms. This is a call to participate in the recreation of a new reality influenced by the much larger matrices of Great Nature and the spirit worlds surrounding the small structure of the house that hasn't completely stood up to the enormity of these powers.

These larger-than-life essences challenge the familiar limits of what is known and has provided comfort to the well-developed identity of waking, provisional, strategic life. The Big Self is more a relative of the nature that we also are, *nature's nature naturing*.

The way the dreamer knows herself and the other woman are looking for her parents is a hint that there is a search for the divine couple taking place for finding balance. The mother and father of the friend in the dream are as the Mother and Father of us all, the God and the Goddess, the divine masculine and divine feminine in conjoined, wedded form. For, *Dream Parents are*, on a very real level, *the ones who gave us life and came here before us*. The search for these personages in the dream suggests the move towards a renewal of the absent masculine, by the previously derogated feminine element so vividly pronounced within the dream. We need only look at the apparent destructiveness towards Mother Earth as depicted in the dream's account of experience, and also in waking life to see this level of the dreams genius revelation. We'll visit this below in greater detail.

Swamps are places of great fecundity and ever-renewing life. Water's presence in the dream brings forth qualities of emotive feeling and fluidity, typifying the way value can be experienced apart from and in addition to thought. The dancing and sultry music further the sensuous aspect of the visions messages of import.

Other aspects of the dream are suggestive of the archetypal energy of rebirth and renewal. In an important way, water in our dreams also re-presents the mythical *Water of Life*. When mothers are close to giving birth, the water breaks and flows out, so here we also have an aid to being born and a hint that the Great Feminine Creatrix is involved in a powerful way in this intriguing recalled nighttime adventure.

FURTHER AMPLIFYING THE DREAM

The word "archetype" as invoked throughout this writing refers to *basic, universal energies and patterns that can be located at all times, for all people, in all places, specifically containing a uniquely psychic, spiritual, physical and soul essence.* The idea of archetypes is a cornerstone of Jungian praxis and goes back at least as far as Plato, in his notion of the "Old Ideas". To refer to the archetypical energy of water, for instance, is to notice the qualities of water that are felt and can be understood by all people across all cultures and in all ages.

Returning to our unfolding of the dream, in the telling, the dreamer notes the snaking quality of the trees and also experiences her skin as "a paper-thin and bloodied bark". In these portions of the dream, one can easily imagine the old mythic renditions of the Tree of Life and the Tree of the Knowledge of Good and Evil. We also may surmise the archetypical presences of the Serpent and Eve in the Garden.

Trees are rooted, enfleshed, stretching, grounded and lofty beings of the earth, able to exist in at least three realms at once – the underland, the middle world, and the heavens. Through experiencing a shared sense of identity in the dream with these arboreal beings, it seems the dreamer is undergoing an expanded realization of a more-than-human identification with *the nature of nature naturing.*

These details evoke a sense of ancient spiritual resonance with trees as a symbol for timeworn growth and renewal in the psyche. Shamanic cultures have related to trees as beings capable of connecting people with the energies of the Other Worlds, the Spirit Realms. From North America to Siberia, in Celtic and African countries people have revered trees as ancestor beings that have their branches, trunks and roots in a variety of spiritual and physical places "all-at-once".

The energy of sharing life-substance with trees echoes the ideas and practices of ancient, spiritual and indigenous cultures in that it metaphorically leaps into an actual experience of relatedness. To wear bark with these plant people is to resonate with the understanding that what is human is not separate; rather, the dream suggests that human nature is akin to the regenerating forces of life as it extends to and from Great Nature. Trees in waking life, dreams and in folk-myths suggest a living memory of the rhythmic dance of existence as held forth by these characters of the natural world who change, wave, sprout, die and grow. Trees also remain standing throughout the seasonal cycles of time. All without going anyplace, rooted to the spot! Trees draw nourishment from below and pull sustenance up into their trunks, eventually feeding windblown and spirit-dancing leaves, invisible visitors and winged creatures in their boughs, holding court with rain, sun and moon. Like trees, we may open to the many powers and beings that co-exist and depend on one another, tending the vibrant inter-relations of being 'betwixt and between' the physical, spiritual and soul aspects of existence. As trees don't appear to move from one place to the next in the way humans do, it can also be said that they offer a lesson about how to belong.

The ever-present awareness of ecological crisis today can be seen in the dream's call to feel the effects of destruction upon ourselves, and our essential cohabitants, that also provide us with the very air we need in order to survive in our relative domains. The motif of apocalypse calls out a level of shared, panhuman experience to show up a largely forgotten truth of interconnection with all of nature. In the modern world, we tend to conceive of nature as a thing outside ourselves, versus a living garment of which we too are woven and needs be responsible towards.

There is also a strong hint of sacred wounding, in the blood and the burnt skin-bark. The dreaming ego experiences being human, plant, element, even animal, in the perception of the trees as being snake-like. This layer symbolizes one of the characteristics of psychic reality, *the nature of the psyche*, found in many dreams, where we can consider that we are also each aspect within the dream itself. The wisdom of dreams and visions expresses its genius in the way it brings seemingly separate layers together without losing important distinctions.

Blood is also worthy of our attention here. Vitality and memory exist in the sanguinary fluids that course through living physical forms. Combining liquid, oxygen and minerals, human blood is blue on the inside and red when exposed to air. In my experience, dream blood almost always has something to say about the life that exists within, as a guiding metaphor of its very function pertaining to our own fleshy existences. Blood is a fluid that bespeaks vigor, movement, physicality and a host of combining essential elements. Without enough of the right kind of blood, life in a physical capacity is not possible for many living beings. Blood also suggests familial ties, both to our immediate kin and our long lines of ancestors.

An experience of serpents is another archetypically valid theme found here, as it relates to the mythological associations surrounding encounters with "creepy-crawlies" and sacred wounds. The snake, a true denizen of the earth, resounds with mythic meanings pertinent to the ongoing cycles of death, rebirth and renewal. Snakes are extremely primal beings. The image of the uroboros in alchemy reminds us that serpent energy is capable of teaching us how *life feeds on death, that which was previously alive,* and will ever remake itself anew through the shedding of its' own living-dying skin.

Consider what Edinger, a Jungian writer who has given us well-elucidated maps of the psyche based on studies in comparative mythology, relates about this energy ,

"The theme of encountering... a snake... in dreams... generally has the same meaning that the succumbing to the serpent in the Garden of Eden had for Adam and Eve; namely, that an old state of affairs is being lost and a new conscious insight is being born."[5]

Thus we see the dream use the language of deeply meaningful and symbolic metaphors to connect us with a further energy of the potent imaginal factors that embody movements towards a transformed identity. Again, we note spiraling layers connected to the apocalyptic theme. For the snake, as encountered in Eden bespoke the "end of an age of innocence" and thereby introduced a new kind of knowledge that heralded the end of a previous order and the beginning of a new one.

A mythic understanding is one that helps shine forth the inherent inevitability of an evolutionary (that is to say *unfolding*) pattern existing between age-old aspects of death and renewal. The serpent energy in the trees, threaded together with the other elements of the dream, strongly suggest a reality wherein endings lead to new beginnings and vice versa. This is the cycle that Eliade called *The Myth of the Eternal Return*. Often – if not always – on one level of the dreams in which these characters appear, there is a representation (as who and what they actually also are!) of the seasonality of the designs of destruction and creation.

Let's also reflect further now upon the blackening of the skin in the dream. Fire has often been associated with the presence of transformational energies. Fire is a prime force that transmutes substances. No other element can do this in the way that fire does. This would seem to tie in with the snake energy, on the level of the shedding of the skin. Some trees actually also shed their bark in a kind of sloughing off of the old to birth the new. The experience of having been "blackened" induces a sense of being cooked, which reminds of the alchemical observations surrounding the *nigredo*. This is the appearance of endarkening shadow material, and the archetypal energy of preparing something for change through heating it up. This is something we do with our food all the time. So, we could also say that an ironic, yet viable, nourishment is being implied in this action of the blackening.

THE RETURN OF THE DARK WOMAN OF THE SOUL

All this leads us to the end of the dream and an encounter with Sheena the Destroyer. As we worked this material in our group, it became clear that this apparent divinity bears a close and familiar resemblance to the Hindu deities Shakti and Shiva, the Destroyer-Creator couple of the East Indian pantheon. Therefore, it further behooves us to seek to stir up these archetypal embodiments of ancient sacred wisdom. Are these our long sought Dream Parents whose presence was announced early in the dream?

In Hindu cosmology Shiva is both Creator and Destroyer. His partner is Shakti, the Cosmic Woman who also embodies these powers. Sheena seems to stand for these qualities in a distinct womanly form. She is clearly recognized as such in the dream. I suspect it is here that we do find the divine parents, the Goddess-God dyad displayed artfully by the dream in diverse, spontaneous, unified and powerful imagery.

What are we to make of this? I suggest, here the dream artfully envisions the imbalance of masculine and feminine energies. Are we witnessing the Great Feminine alone here? Or is She, somehow, also being accompanied by the Great Masculine in the dream? The very name "Sheena" smacks of a dream wordplay on the names Shiva and Shakti. "Sheena" sounds almost like "Shiva" yet the dream features this divinity as a womanly person. A literalist view will never do if we want to discover the path towards wholeness.

Consider the following in relation to this issue of balance between Shakti and Shiva from Indian writer Pradip Bhattacharya,

"The Oriya tradition of Bhubaneswar goes against any feminist interpretation: without Shiva, Shakti cannot create, on her own she destroys society and nature. While in terms of physiology man is superior, in terms of culture women surpass men. The Goddess power is significant only when reigned from within... to Oriya women... the male and female deities are not just side by side but even within each other... in the world of the Goddess separation is illusory and founded in a profound unity at its core."[6]

In this rendering, we behold an acknowledged potential paradoxical inseparability between the very divine personages and energies in question. This is a tenet of traditional tantric practice, as well as that of the ancient Celts, who state that "in every man there is a woman and in every woman there is a man".

The aim of many sacred practices, and earthly endeavors, is the uniting of these apparently set apart forces of man and woman. Indeed, the teachings of Jungian psychology also revolve around the understanding that in order to seek to achieve wholeness, people will want to unite these seemingly and actually opposed yet ultimately conjoined, complimentary powers. For a long list of reasons, it seems that human consciousness has been oriented, over time, at separating these energies. We see this in the Christian tradition and through other cultures, at least in the Western world, where the masculine outweighs the feminine. Just think of the Holy Trinity, which traditionally doesn't have a place for Mother Mary within it. The dream here seems to be pointing out a way that it's possible, according to our deep natures, and nature's depth of being, that the two are actually also one.

In comparing Sheena to Shakti, it's of great interest that, as Bhattacharya says, the Goddess without the God wreaks only destruction. Along with the semi-waking dialogue that the dreamer engaged in with Sheena, this indicates to my heart and mind, how one implication of the dream relates to finding a way to bring forth a viable masculine form of being, alongside and within the feminine.

When I imagine this dream of *Sheena the Destroyer* for myself, the dream presents this all important spiritual theme as it relates to the depth of my experience as a collectively related individual living in a time of great destruction, separation and opposition. Sheena announces that I too share an inseparable identity with the larger-than-life feminine-masculine energies of archetypal nature, which inherently includes all the struggles of humanity – death, disease and destruction. Sheena herself, and the varied energetic forces of the dream depict the old world coming apart. Out of that ending a call to acknowledge the destruction-creation of a new reality (based on and connected with the old one) is heralded by her arising out of and returning to the depths.

Sheena is feminine, on the one hand, because these are the missing, fierce, womanly and undervalued qualities of the day and of many ages. In the lopsided world of a severely over-pronounced intellectual and reasonable approach to life, which appears to have humankind (and hundreds of other species!) teetering on the edge of destruction, these feminine values and characteristics must be embodied. And here they are rising out of the rich loam of the life-giving, life-taking swamplands in the dream.

There is also a move here towards an authentic balanced masculine nature. This can be understood by extension of Bhattacharya's description of Shiva-Shakti. The message of the dream indicates that the feminine in the masculine, and vice versa, is powerfully demanding to be brought together as inseparable. Because the dreamer herself uses a "dream-sword" to cut Sheena into pieces, we can say that *here is the decidedly masculine element* – imaged as a blade. These energies in the psyche are not gender-bound, in a literal sense. So let us not make the mistake that some form of unhelpful sexism is at play here.

Blades of any variety in the dreamworld, and hence in the psyche, are metaphorical and symbolic arbiters of the energy of sharpness - that which cuts and bears potential for distinction as a result of its very purpose. The action of cutting Sheena up is strongly suggestive of the ability to make such action-oriented distinctions.

Why is Sheena in Destroyer-mode? On a key level, this is tied to what Bhattacharya has said above. Where is the masculine collaboration here? Sheena comes as a destructive force, in part, because her ally and complementary male side is missing in action – masculinity has divided itself against the feminine in the collective waking world and so she becomes a devouring force. It's as if she's saying, the false order must be cut away in favor of a more collaborative approach. The crucial, repressed feminine must rise up and she does so in the dream to make known this all-important fact. The masculine archetype of cutting distinction is necessary (as invoked by the feminine), for what isn't working to be destroyed and for renewal to occur – even where the literalized masculine is too much in power. The dream shows the feminine being cut down, a possible depiction of the destructiveness of a one-sided view. We could imagine that the sword is also used to cut down the prior unworkable form, which inevitably leads to a much-needed renewal. So the masculine is also involved here as well. This is all very subtle and paradoxical.

The out of control masculine has its own destructive effects. However, these would appear to exist more like extinction than renewable destructiveness. The denial of the creative-destructive energies seems to have taken place with this imbalanced masculine energy at the helm. For this reason, Sheena appears – the Sacred Woman – to ironically show that naturally, cosmically ordered modes of acknowledged death and suffering are part of the fabric of existence. In the modern western world, we could see that the masculine forces, as witnessed through war and medical advancement, seek to misguidedly prolong and sustain life – often through exported forms of destruction that harm others in the effort to protect. Unfortunately, the opposite of this intended aim is often the ultimate effect. This is where part of the imbalance lies. It's as if everything is turned backwards. By denying the rhythms of actual death and renewal as evoked and inherently held forth by the matrices of the natural order, all efforts to uphold life alone are doomed to seemingly hidden and enormously impacting forces.

BALANCING THE ONE AND THE MANY

This is another fascinating aspect of working with dreams. In my experience they always contain exacting yet expansive messages for the individual dreamer, and they also illustrate, in potent and creative forms, what is out of kilter within the human and beyond-human collectives at the same time. In various mythologies the world over, feminine aspects of the divine incarnate at exactly these moments when human beings go off course, the Great Forgetters, who, with much effort and great fortune, may also become the Great Rememberers. In Egyptian mythos, we might recall the lioness aspect of the sun god Ra, known as Sekhmet. She may also be a relative of Sheena.

Ra released Sekhmet upon the Egyptians when they decided that they had everything they needed to shine, without any need for paying homage to the solar deity as the true and mighty source of actual light in the world. How like our hubristic times today this is! In the tale, the lion-goddess in her wrathful manifestation sets about devouring people and an enormous bloodbath ensues. This energy is also present in Sheena as she appears through a spontaneous production of the dreaming source in a raucously similar fashion. She does so, I suggest, to remind us of the import of seeking balance and honoring spirit, the earthly yet divine powers of creation and destruction, as well as material reality. The need to brandish a kind of righteous anger as a confrontation with renewal and restoration is visible in both Sheena's appearance and the old myth of Sekhmet. I suspect the ancient Egyptians were also somehow out of relation with the Womanly Powers when Sekhmet came onto the scene. This is the

Dark Feminine who appears to round life out when it becomes one-sided.

The dream solicits an appropriate sense of fear in the presence of this figure. Sheena is a representative of a very profound force in the psyche, the spirit realms and the vital living physical world in front of our eyes.

As the interwoven energies in this dream powerfully propose, we are all the characters and energies in the dreams, on one important level – because we're all related and interdependent. I love the vulnerability of the dreamer that I perceive in her perspicacious engagement with Sheena just upon bareley waking. This is what Jungians would call an Active Imagination. It takes the meeting to a more consciously relational level.

In the dialogue, Sheena confirms several of the associations we've already outlined here. She reminds us of the life-death-life cycle and paints a vivid portrait of wholeness by demanding that life is a form of work, struggle and suffering, as well as about death and dying.

When I see myself as the dreamer undergoing the action of cutting Sheena to pieces, it strikes me that I have become the destroyer. I am willingly taking the message I've been gifted by the dream and embody it by participating in enacting the fierce move of destroying the goddess herself and returning her to where she came from. This might seem like a re-enactment of the relegation of the feminine to the underlands. And yet, we can also say that by cutting her up, one recognizes that there is a right place for the divinity in relationship to humanity. It's like Sudama and Krishna once more. The dream says there truly is no fully destroying the goddess. Rather, one aspect of her being exists in the ability to die and be reborn, and the very act of cutting Sheena up and watching her fall back in to the swamp is a deep honoring of this energy in oneself and the world.

The work with this dream, as heartily elaborated here, is very much like the work we do in groups and individual sessions. We *amplify* the dream material. We find and draw parallels that exist in mythology and based on known archetypal resonance in the dream work to flesh out the possible messages of experience for anyone who is willing to participate. Such a dream is of great interest to all of us, I would say. This import arrives in the way the dream-tale displays energies and figures, who appear in our dreams, that we may have never directly encountered in the waking world, yet which can be clearly identified in various folk traditions, dreams and mythologies throughout time. This visit from such beings in dreams strongly supports their autonomous existence and validates verifiable soul and spirit realities who exist apart from the human ego or personality.

Endnotes, Chapter 2

[1] John Ayto, "The Dictionary of Word Origins", Arcade Publishing, New York, 2011, p.277

[2] Martin Shaw, "A Branch from the Lightning Tree, Ecstatic Myth and the Grace in Wildness", White Cloud Press, Ashland Oregon, 2011, p.113

[3] Marie-Louise von Franz, "Projection and Re-Collection in Jungian Psychology, Reflections of the Soul", Open Court, Chicago and La Salle, 1995, p. 82

[4] Diane Farris, Jeremy Taylor, "Dream Images, A Portfolio of Photographs and Dream Symbols", Blurb.com self-publishing, 2012, p.20

[5] Edward Edinger, "Ego and Archetype", Shambala, Boston & London, 1992, p.21

[6] Pradip Bhattacharya, review of "Is the Goddess a Feminist?" in "International Journal of Hindu Studies", Volume 8, Number 1-3, January 2004, p. 205

CHAPTER 3

This Darkness is the Lighthouse

"There is no 'Them', only 'Us', only me and you"
Bono

From a down-to-earth perspective, no world-view can be complete without an on-going consideration about the reality of the human and archetypal Shadow, both bright and dark.

Because of its very character, the conversation about such energy can become hard to track. Shadow has much to do with the unknown, so we can talk of shadow in relation to the not-yet-speech-ripe. Since such energies dwell in the darkened rooms of consciousness, great effort, awareness and finesse are required to make contact of a helpful sort with them.

In his book, *Why Good People Do Bad Things*, James Hollis describes the thing itself thus,

"What we call the Shadow… is the sum total of all those separate energies that operate unconsciously, and therefore autonomously, or that are an affront to what we consciously wish to think of ourselves."[1]

Just like the dark echo-shape of the body that shifts upon the ground nearby, the Shadow varies according to the conditions that help to shape it. Its form is, in part, influenced by the way we bring it into our gaze of consciousness. Shadow is necessarily always also going to remain what it inherently is, in and of itself. As with one's literal physical shadow, these dark forms exist whether we are looking at them or not.

Since we live in a daytime reality that is composed of various degrees of shadow and light, these physical yet psychic forces tend to be a constant feature of our visual, felt and bodily experience. It's been said that we can't know the darkness without the light.

Let's be clear, so as not to call forth an unhelpful shadow energy here. Dark does not equal bad, nor does light equal good, in any concrete fashion. If we think in terms of the symbolic resonance of day and night, we understand that what is in the light tends to be known and identifiable. The darkness of nighttime may arouse fear or curiosity. The nightworld surely limits our capacity to see and know what is contained within it. Yet this quality in and of itself, is not necessarily harmful. Too much light can also burn things up, or create a "white-out" that blinds everything from view. Too much darkness may also become troubling if there is a great amount of obscurity covering what needs to be known and seen.

The fact that each day is followed by a night suggests that both dark and light are needed ingredients here in this waking world.

At times, ideas and projections around shadow have been mistakenly literalized where we have sought to create judgmental distinctions that manifest as racism. The way we image our individual and collective shadow energies reveals much about the unknown and misplaced energy that exists within us. It's important to recognize that both Bright and Dark Shadow energies hold helpful and harmful capacities. The practice of working with the Shadow is not meant as a "black and white" framework for simply assigning creative or destructive identities to light and dark entities or people. Our dreams suggest how we all embody the entire spectrum of hurtful and harmonizing possibilities, and so much more. Therefore, we would do well to explore our unexamined notions about the value of the light, the dark, and all their variegated combinations.

In the interest of entering the conversation with the presence of soul, let's invoke a poetic portal into the Shadow by considering William Stafford's *The Way It Is*. (Best read aloud!)

> " There is a thread you follow, it goes among things that change, but it doesn't change.
>
> People ask about what you are pursuing, you have to explain about the thread, but it isn't easy for others to see.

While you hold it you can't get lost.

Tragedies happen, people get sick and die, we suffer and grow old, nothing we do can stop the unfolding of time.

We don't ever let go of the thread."

In a very real way, Shadow is the thread. May we hold this fibrous lifeline throughout the conversation here, so we don't become unhelpfully lost.

The metaphorical and actual nature of the Shadow carries forth in dreams and the psyche as the essence of energies that are unknown, mysterious and can be said to be seen and felt as within yet beyond the current bounds of attention.

Robert Bly has spoken of the shadow as all the layers of unlived life within our selves and within existence. In essence, shadow contains all the as-yet-unexpressed energies of what we might consider to be helpful, favorable, destructive, hurtful, paradoxical or benign possibilities.

"Wait", I can hear you saying, "This sounds almost exactly like the earlier description of the unconscious or the unknown". True, these energies and realties are very wrapped up in one another. Yet the ascribing of shadowy qualities to certain aspects of experience helps us to more clearly image, know and talk about the way unknown and put-back-together portions of our beings appear in our dreams and in waking life. We could say that shadow is an integral, even personable aspect of the great mysterious.

A sheer physical imagining of shadows involves the way that bodies, people, animals, mountains, trees, clouds, cities, all and more, can be seen to cast imprints of shapes in the form of darkened patterns. These castings become visible relative to emanations of light pouring forth from a host of sources, including the sun, moon, stars and electric energies of human-harnessed creations.

Maybe we tend to think primarily of the shadow as that shape seen in the composition that is described upon the ground underneath us. Yet, what of the shadowed territory that exists between the body and the ground? If I'm standing outside in the mid-morning and the sun is shining in the sky, I can look to see where my shadow lands upon the earth. The shadow-form that appears beneath me only describes *a portion* of my actual shadow. The space between my body and that outline also contains my shadow-stuff. I can witness this when I put my hand in that zone, recognizing that it no longer carries the light in the way that it did before I placed it there. In the realm between myself and my shadow, my hand darkens, and I can sense that something of my being has been placed into a twilight zone which I experience as much less palpable than the traceable pool of darkness which is spread out upon the surface below.

Shadows, particularly the ones we cast ourselves, follow and mimic us wherever we go, whatever we do. We cannot simply decide not to relate to shadows. No matter how hard we try, we cannot will them away. One could go into complete darkness, as on a night when the moon seems to have disappeared forever, to seek to dissolve the private shadow, yet when we do so, we are engulfed in an enormous shade that seems to amplify our own individual shape into an endless ocean of silhouette. It's also true that the brighter the light that casts a shadow, the darker that shadow becomes.

SHADOW IN PSYCHE, PSYCHE IN SHADOW

One of the reasons that ideas about Shadow are so important, is that these physical experiences of shadows embody, symbolically and actually, the way psychic shadows act and exist in both a psychological and spiritual fashion in non-ordinary, subtle space, in dreams and visionary states – in the psyche and imaginal realms – and thereby, in the daylit world.

In stories shadows appear as ghosts, dark mages and bewildering animals cloaked in black, as raven sometimes does, in the forested woods beneath a silvery moon that hangs across from the setting sun. In dreams, shades dress up in such likely garb and as dark people or energies that are often as-yet-unidentifiable and which echo the characteristics of the dreamer in significant ways. Shadow in dreams is also often featured as scenarios that take place in fecund, excrement-laden toilets and in the personages of killers and powerful, frightening, mighty beasts.

Nature has its shadows too. These may appear in the form of ice storms, earthquakes, tidal waves, volcanic blasts, poisonous creatures, floods, fires and epidemic illnesses. Shadow is, on one level, the expression of the Life-Death-Life cycle. The more we push it away, judge and ignore it, the more we tend to experience shadow as a harmful, troublesome and threatening force to be eradicated.

Today, a large portion of collective shadow can be seen as it relates to the ongoing voracious destruction of nature in the name of "progress". A grievous lack of awareness of what we have been doing to ourselves and the earth, has culminated in the ever-growing ecological crisis of our era. Throughout the recent Industrial Revolution, people seem to have been unaware of the natural limits around the impact of human actions upon people, the living beings of the wood, the thirst-slaking rains, the cloud-filled skies, the mountain crags, teeming meadows and fecundating soils.

At one time, not so long ago, it may have been considered that Nature was too vast to be able to be wounded beyond repair. As recently as in the past couple hundred years, a common thought seems to have been that if a society decided to relegate its waste to the nearby ocean waters, the sea itself was so huge that it would be able to cleanse itself from any materials given to it to swallow up. I believe this was the case with the San Francisco Bay in California, where toxic wastes were dumped regularly in the 1800's and early 20th Century. This perception seems to have contributed to the incessant cutting down of trees throughout the forests of the world as well. The conventional thought seems to have been that it would all grow back, so why worry about taking too much when there was more than enough to go around?

When we look with hindsight, we can know that this is and was not the case. Just a few days ago I saw a heart-achingly mournful photo of an emaciated polar bear out on the ice. This struggling creature's coat hangs off of an undernourished frame of ghostly bones. We've known this was coming for some time. As the ozone holes continue to grow in magnitude, and the climate changes across the planet, we might do well to recognize that what we don't know *can* hurt us, the vital living creatures, and the world in which we dwell. It turns out that ignorance is not bliss, after all.

The issues that grow out of collective and individual shadow energies can be understood as connected to a human predisposition, so rife today, towards seeking to eliminate the unknowns in our experience.

> Taylor once more,
> "The global industrial 'war on nature' is actually… an unconsciously projected and thoroughly misguided war on the unconscious itself… It makes no more rational sense to talk about 'winning' any war in this postmodern era than it does to talk about 'winning an earthquake' or 'winning a wildfire'."[2]

In terms of the effect of shadow energy, we need only look at our history of exacting war and destruction upon one another, the earth and ourselves, which continues to rage around and within us in the modern world. Clear manifestations of repressed shadow energies include the Nazi Holocaust, as well as the mostly unacknowledged Holocaust on Women during the not-too-distant time of the Witch Hunts in the eastern united states. In these instances, untold numbers of human beings suffered terribly at the hands of other human beings seeking to supposedly "make the world a better place".

In North America, mass genocide forms the historical backdrop for the creation of an essentially European culture supposedly valuing spiritual and human liberty above all else. The records are there for all to see how the Native Peoples of this place were intentionally made sick, hunted and killed to make room for settlers from abroad and out of fear about "the strange ways" of people who lived quite differently than those arriving from across the Great Waters. How could such a culture of exiles as ours ever rationalize the mass murder and rape of men, women and children as a viable route to religious freedom? Literalized destruction, according to history and experience, can be found not to honor the freedom of anyone, in the end. In fact, such ignorance may more accurately be seen as a manifestation of the refusal and inability to work with shadow energies as they appear in the human psyche and in the world.

More recently we could point out the tension that exists between "legal" Americans and immigrants from South of the Border. In Arizona and the southern states there is a long lived out battle between the previous wave of European immigrants and the people who come to North America to do the work that most European descendants would rather not do for themselves, yet which we depend upon.

On the other side of the coin, if we can see instances of how the unlived potentials for destruction live within us and in our world, we may also see that the same or greater potentials also exist for helpfully and imaginatively engaging our lives in such a way that we might call forth our greatest gifts and healing capacities. It is often these Bright Shadow energies that can be even more difficult to recognize.

> " When the creative energies of the Bright Shadow are 'expressed' only in projected form, at the very least it has a direct, negative influence on cultural innovation, which in turn exercises a negative influence on the development of further conscious awareness in countless individuals. When bright shadow energies are withdrawn, and given concrete expression, the lives of individuals and whole societies are transformed."[3]

It may seem paradoxical that this would be the case. However, we might gain some understanding if we consider, in our own lives, how have we failed to fully express the creative viabilities we know we are each capable of? Can we honestly ask ourselves, are we currently living these powers in the world? What Taylor describes above, has to do with the tendency to see our own capacity for expressing our gifts as they appear in others. One praises heroes and heroines, expecting their greatness, while cheerleading from a safe distance. Yet, the invitation is to fully live such energies in and for our selves. Then, they can have an effect on and for others as well, instead of forever residing in a select elevated few.

I don't know that we've seen too many folks step into this energy and become extremely visible in the last few eras. Maybe we just haven't heard much about them. Lately, people are toting Pope Francis as a kind of revolutionary and unexpected force in the Catholic world. Many seem to have hoped that Barack and Michelle Obama would contain and act out our Bright Shadow potentials for us.

My mind and heart go to more unlikely examples of folks living what we can call an everyday existence, to seek examples of the way these forces can effect important change. I think of Rosa Parks and her simple yet courageous willingness to demand a proper seat for herself as an older black woman on a city bus. She flew in the face of major dark shadow projections at a time when racism was perhaps more clearly out in the open, by insisting to sit in the "white" section because of her poorly health and personal verve. I suspect that on some level she also may have been fed up with the ignorance she no doubt encountered on a daily basis.

I've met several young, middle aged and older males in men's gatherings that have reflected a radical willingness to live and own dark and bright shadow materials. These men may never become "well-known" for their actions. Former (and current) gang bangers, prison inmates and social-spiritual activists I was privileged to witness in these settings took hard and honest looks at their wounds and were equally encouraged to notice the gifts that sat right next to the scars. I myself was emboldened to see the gifts hidden in my wounds in the initiatory container we all entered together in the Northern California Redwoods, and eventually ended up becoming more deeply involved in my dream work practice as well as community volunteer mentoring as a result. Those experiences and the people connected to them are with me as I sit down and write, as I am now, when I would rather avoid the task of working hard to find ways to communicate these ideas.

It may be easier to identify the downsides, problems, tragedies and hurts than to actually step into being and becoming the people we know we can be. Doesn't it seem that most speak of the dark shadows more so than the bright ones? Pick up any newspaper and note the tone of dark shadow versus bright. Something about staying focused on what isn't working may allow us to remain overly broken, splintered and disengaged. In standing back and pointing out the issues, we might attempt to keep our hands clean, while not taking the chance to see how our own unique offerings could provide much needed assistance to others, as well as how our own disavowing of the darkness contributes to hardship. This all requires something from us, a kind of sacrifice - a 'making sacred' -and very likely a healthy dose of humility balanced by some well called for courage.

When we own and inhabit our bright shadows, our unlived boons, that claim requires some devotion to risk ourselves with one another and in full view of the communities we move in. This involves a willingness to fail at what we're good at. Expressing our genuine selves means opening our hearts to being broken, to moments wherein we may see and feel what and who we love get hurt.

It's deeply important to raise our aware consciousness of both the darkness and the light, within and without. Once we become more akin to these energies, we often find that they present us with real choices about how we could live our lives.

BACKING UP TO THE PERSONAL SHADOW

Dreams reliably show us where we are in relation to these energies as they show up in our own beings. It's possible to speak of the strictly *personal*, as compared to the *collective* or *archetypal shadow* .

The shady experiences of a lifetime get stored in the backroom of the private shadow. These relate to our own independent histories that we co-author as individuals in this lifetime.

To give a personal example, I could talk about my tendency towards shyness. Being shy may not seem so shadowy, yet it does describe a way that one can tend to withhold capacities for life and for expressing the gifts that we can know we came to this life to offer. For me, shyness connects at times to laziness and also melancholy. Sometimes, shyness acts as a front for anger and unclaimed doses of grandiosity. Claiming shyness may allow a person to protect oneself unduly and to avoid fully risking an attempt to powerfully act and be within the world. At times my dreams tend to reflect this by putting me in scenarios with others wherein I seek to distract myself from the tasks of truly being seen and witnessed, which the people of my dreaming advents appear to want to attract me towards.

This played out in the dreamtime as a recent dinner date with an exotic woman in her family restaurant in New York, who I dodge in the dream. At other times, I find myself being chased or hunted by shady characters, which I seek to escape. This activity is usually a tip off, for any of us dreaming these scenes that some vital life energy is reaching out to us in the dream world in an effort to bring us more fully alive. I see this in others dreams too. If the many folks I work with who have similar "A-ha's" are any indication, this phenomenon holds for many of us, not just myself. Another line from poet David Whyte in his dream-blessing poem *What to Remember When Waking* goes, "To be human is to become visible, carrying what is hidden as a gift to others."

The *personal shadow* energies appear in relationships where we "act out" inherited reactions and compensatory behaviors reflexively gained through formative personal history, such as in familial settings. In an openly abusive family, one might add a quality of bullish aggression to one's bag of personal shadow materials. Others, raised in "nice families" may learn to act more like quietly coiled vipers, who only strike when least expected. Whatever the exact characteristics, we all develop personal shadow qualities through the courses of our lives, whether we come from raucously abusive backgrounds or seemingly smooth-sailing homes or some derivative in between. Whatever collections of shadow we gain as children tend to adapt as a lifetime unfolds.

In many people's dreams, scenes involving bathrooms, toilets, and various forms of excrement, are a reliable indicator that one is up against some level of shadow material in the psyche, both personal and collective. Toilets and baths are places where, at least for Western folk, we tend to do some of the most private and "dirty" things that we engage in as human beings. Symbolically and actually, urine and feces typify the energy of the shadow. These "waste materials" are the product of biological, mostly unseen, symbolic and transformative movements in the body. For various obvious reasons, they also represent materials that are experienced as "nasty" and "dangerous". Biologically, it behooves us to relate to these materials carefully, as they can make us sick when mishandled. These forms help us to image how we tend to view and experience certain energies in our selves and in life, as well as how our feelings and attitudes can be realized in relation to the dramatic, seemingly mundane, "shitty" or "pissy" energies in our waking lives, dreams and fantasies.

It's also true that feces can be *fecund*. Many forms of manure are natural fertilizers that have the ability to bring renewal forth via the very jaws of destruction. Urine itself, it may seem strange to know, has been used at various points throughout time as a deeply sacred form of 'liquid gold', as a healing elixir. To merely suggest such ideas may evoke feelings of repugnance for those of us who have had little contact with such realities. We could say that this brings up the personal and or collective, shared shadow, in that case.

Dream toilets, peeing, pooping and so forth, in the dream world at least, are indicative of the wasted and trying energies that we tend to hold in and keep to ourselves. Releasing, being aware of, recycling, properly disposing of and relating to these energies is a potent and ever-returning symbolic re-presentation of the very energies we encounter as humans that we find most troubling. Dreams evoke such images to depict psycho-spiritual energies embodying the forces we have had the most difficulty recognizing as belonging to us and our neighbors. The potentials of energy and action that are symbolized in this way also reveal our attitudes, ideas, feelings and experiences around the "worst things" in our lives and the most awful outcomes we can imagine. These are shadow energies *par excellence*!

In the ancient tradition of Alchemy, the mystical spiritual art practiced in Europe as the shadow of conventional Christian religion, Jung revealed that "shit" was the actual material for the beginning, the *primal material,* of what alchemists call "the work" or "the opus". This effort would be the equivalent pursuit of what Jung came to call "individuation", meaning "undivided". In Eastern language and practice these terms could be compared and contrasted with the "search for enlightenment". In alchemy, waking life and in dreams, it appears that such a quest involves an *endarkenment.*

Alchemy has been shown to go back at least to the time of the archaic Egyptians and, in that culture, had much to do with the arts of death, burial and embalming. These ancients were also known to use urine as a liquid anointing material under special conditions! Inner and outer work can be shown to involve the "dark matter" of our lives, what we tend to speak of as "all the shit we have to deal with". Apparently, the great effort of transformation in alchemical practice was bound up with devotions that sought to transmute dark matter, the *nigredo* or *massa confusa* into its brightened aspect by going imaginatively into the darkness itself. *Dark matter* is most often the very thing that is being thrown away, or flushed down the toilet and is considered worthless to the majority.

The notion here is that it's possible, even necessary, to reveal the undiscovered riches that inherently exist in the hastily devalued darkness as a path towards wholeness. It turns out that, hidden within the off-putting waste materials of our lives, there exists the potential for alchemical gold. In various turns of phrase, we find this same energy spoken of as "the diamond in the rough", "the treasure hard to attain" and "the pearl of great price". Be it gold, jewel or diverse treasure, such riches are said to only be attainable through the engagement with a "dark night of the soul". Such transformation occurs through a willing surrender to dark energies and an ability to witness, relate to and reach for the glories of spectacularly distant and heavenly, no longer existing stars in the overwhelmingly blackened spaciousness of the nighttime skies. In a sense, to find the light, we seem to need to travel through dark realms and to learn the lessons held there first. Would the nighttime sky be so beautiful, the stars so compelling, if it all wasn't held together by so much shadow?

The Personal Shadow descends into and connects towards what we call the Collective Shadow. These seemingly separate levels of shadow can be seen, at some point, to overlap. This deeper, universal, shared layer of the psyche reflects a quality of human potential and more-than-human actuality that can be seen to reflect qualities belonging to all of humankind as well as to the cosmos. We could say that tendencies such as jealousy, self-centered interests, grandiosity, hatred, as well as dehumanization, and a fearful, destructive attitude towards Great Nature reside in the Collective Dark Shadow. Each shadow quality has its favorable and unfavorable sides. All such qualities may be witnessed and manifest personally and with certain idiosyncratic tones, yet also may be further identified as arising out of much larger, archetypal realties and manifest in groups in larger societies. Perhaps we can develop a kind of "second sight", in this sense, honoring both sides of the coins of shadow, jealousy as a relative of desire, self-centeredness as a kind of centered self, hatred as the other cheek on the face of love.

SHADOW CANNIBALS AND THE PATH TO AWAKENING

The following dream, graciously provided by a fellow dreamer, raises some clearly depicted motifs we have been considering thus far. The way the dream condenses several ideas that appear to be true about dreams reveals the genius of the dreaming source.

"If I Don't Know What They Mean,
They'll Boil and Eat Me!"

"I'm in a dense jungle. I come upon a tribe of indigenous people who look threatening and are holding spears. They guide me to a cooking pot full of boiling soup in the center of their village and tell me that if I don't figure out what they mean, I will become a main ingredient in their meal! I feel a sense of urgency to figure it all out and just as they are hitting their spears on the ground and preparing to put me in the pot, I suddenly realize that the way I symbolize them has put me in this situation. I awaken and feel greatly relieved that I figured it out before it was too late"... End of Dream.

When I first heard this dream, I burst out laughing at the tricky way it includes a form of commentary about the way the dreamer, and myself in my inevitable projections onto the dream, conceive of these wild, primal people and the parallel situations reflected here.

The dreamer finds herself in a jungle, an earthy locale with many surprising and hard-to-know forces nestled within it, behind leafs, under roots on the tangled ground and in shaded canopies overhead. If this was my dream, in my own imagination of it, I find myself in a teeming place of primal energy, undergoing a confrontation with an ancient people that exist in the spirit worlds of the Dreaming as relatives of my own being. In a jungle it's hard to be aware of all the forces that are thriving and humming, thrumming and hissing, flapping and growing in the labyrinthine surrounds. This setting speaks to a kind of all-encompassing nature-shadow. In this dream forest is much that the dreamer, as a modern western person is likely not to be aware of – a cornucopia of as-yet-unlived-life and death remembered and freshly encountered in the dreamscape.

As contemporary people, living in highly technologized domains, most of us likely hold certain indigenous people and realities hostage in our minds and hearts. We unknowingly bind them to the personal and collective shadow as a sheer result of the relatively recent move by our societies towards civility. When portions of personal and collective experience are devalued or neglected, as the wild side of our own human natures have been and continue to be, we can say that these aspects have *fallen into the Shadow*. Hence, in my version of this dream, I find that I am being faced by the indigenous beings and beingness that I also am.

The "natives" that want to cook me in their soup put a kind of riddle to me, so that I can learn from my relationship to and with them – my own native selves. In a very real fashion, these are the spirits and the World Soul calling me to come into communion with crucial portions of my own connection to nature. One of their important messages is that who and how I am is a source of food to them. I suspect that their query to me about who they are and how I view them is a demand to either feed them with my unknowing, or with my recognition. If I remain unconscious of who and what they are, they'll cook and eat me. On the other hand, if I can understand our interwoven relation with one another, this 'coming to consciousness' will become a call to awakening which requires my further sharing of the experience of the dream as another form of sustenance for these very real people and energies, and for any who would listen to the dream-story's profound messages.

It seems that these wily dream people are asking for an awareness of the unhelpful way in which "the Native" is understood and imagined. Because of the threat in the dream, it's fair to say that this scenario paints a picture wherein these energies want to communicate that if greater knowledge about how these people are being viewed can be gained, the seemingly untoward conclusion can be made known and another outcome can be co-created. Might this be reminiscent of the current dilemma we face around climate change? The dream seems to be asking for a lucid and felt realization about how these apparently primal forces have come to present a threat because of how they are being imagined. This is a way the dreams have of challenging lop-sided ways of knowing people and situations based on the tendency to think their identity is already known. The dream seems to upend such assumptions. Once this insight is gained, relief appears in the form of wakefulness. In essence, the dream comes to show up the way that some essential being has been previously avoided, and yet, now this energy can be squarely faced and related to on every level, as evoked by the dream and its' teaching story of experience.

When it comes to shadow energies and the belonging (the indigenosity, we could say) that the soul is seeking after, these realities will be held hostage by the very gaze that we cast upon them. Once we can shift our conscious viewpoint, the missing pieces fall in to place. This is why it's so fruitful to engage in work with the Shadow – that which we think will destroy us actually holds the missing ingredients for our full sense of being and belonging within its very nature.

Because this dream features "indigenous people", it's my sense that it's communicating something important about how to embody these quite real spirit beings of the soul. An unfortunate bequeathing of the modern stretch towards ever-increasing forms of technology, which the dream seems to counter with its overall feel and tone, is a kind of untrue division between spirit, soul, body, creation, destruction, culture and nature. These wild ones in the dream who show an interest in cooking and eating the dreamers very own organically wrought physical form suggests a call to return to the body. This can be witnessed in the native's request to be understood accurately by the dreamer as living though spirited bodies and entities.

The dreamers timely "A-ha" around this has the fortunate effect of protecting her own dreambody from being boiled and eaten in the dream. A kind of accord is struck through the understanding that all of this has occurred as a result of the way in which people and bodies have previously been understood, felt and thought about, as typified by the dreamer being "let off the hook" after her realization about how she is symbolizing these figures occurs. Upon awakening, the dreamer herself knowingly comes back into her body as well. In other words, the dream suggests that these wild forest people are actively asking to be known for who and what they are: real spirit beings, at the very least relative to the dreamer and the projects of a lifetime.

Carl Jung makes the following statement pertaining to the ways we have of avoiding the body,

> "The thing people are most afraid of is not so much the soul, which to them is practically non-existent, but the body. That is what they don't want to see, the animal or … evil spirit that is waiting to say something to them when they are alone… The body is darkness, and very dangerous things could be called up." [4]

Jung's reference to darkness here could be understood as shadow. In light of his observation, and along with the realties arising out of this dream, it seems possible to say that one of the implications of the story it weaves is to bring body, soul and awareness together, along with what is "indigenous" and "human". The dream involves us in an understanding of how the way we conceive of real energies in our world and each other, as well as in our own beings, can be brought together. This results in a weaving of the imaginal and the physical. We might co-create this embodiment, the dream seems to suggest, in the interest of feeding that which might otherwise feed upon us – seeking to bring life fully back to life, out of a real yet symbolic, initiatory confrontation with a kind of death. This might be done through the efforts of sheer awareness, yet also needs be brought into the body. The dream beseeches recognizing symbolic realities, so that such gleanings might benefit the wild and indigenous people and forces that we also are, deep within and without. After all, to be indigenous is to know where and how the one and the many originate from, to what and who we are indebted for that which feeds us and the larger dream we too are a part of. As humans, we clearly belong to our bodies, on one important level. The *embodiment* of spirit and soul may be our further human task, and a deeper implication of the language and circumstances of this dream.

THE GARDEN ENTRUSTED TO YOU

The cannibal dream raises some intriguing aspects of the issues pertaining to what it might mean to belong to a place, to be and feel and act as if the one and the many are equally "at home" here on planet earth, in our relative little corners of the world.

Unsavory and shadowy qualities in others make a good screen for our projections, so the same energies that exist in us, can land 'out there'. If we turn our attention to homeless people on the streets of America, isn't it interesting that a culture composed primarily of exiles who migrated from our own previous homelands, due to a desire to flee various structures of oppression and warfare as they occurred in Europe, could be so unawares of the tendency to turn around and do the same to others. What I mean is, to be European, and American is to carry a whole inheritance of lost roots in the long bag of shadows that we drag behind us, to invoke Bly's potent metaphor for the shadow. An entire social structure in America has been predicated on a history of fleeing from homelessness, exile and suffered oppression. And yet, how is it that Americans have really acted any differently towards the people we've encountered, in seeking a home and freedom in this "brave new world" known as the United States? It's like the biblical notion of how "the sins of the fathers are visited upon the sons", though we could include mothers and daughters here too.

Where are America's roots, really? And, how is it that a people who have fled our own former sense of belonging in the interest of finding freedom can ignore the fact that we've produced a society where increasing numbers of individuals are not be able to find a home? How many of us alive today in America really feel as if we truly belong anywhere, let alone here? How can we claim a sense of place, when most of us don't even know where our families lived or what they worked at as recently as two or three generations ago? How much of a sense do we really have around what sustains us and gives us life? Where does our food come from and what goes into growing, feeding and caring for it? Are we not a tribe of lost wanderers, who can easily be considered to be homeless ourselves, on some deep and important level, like the people we encounter on the streets and beneath the bridges of our high speed cities? Most of us don't even know the names, qualities and characteristics of the wild animals and plants that inhabit the few remaining forests of this once verdant continent, or among the parks and backyards of our overly domesticated and mostly poorly cared for so-called homes.

Old maps from the late 1800's and early 1900's show how all of North America (also known as Turtle Island by Native Americans) was once covered in rolling swaths of diverse woodlands. Today, only a few skinny patches of green remain on forestry maps, designating the homes of trees across the continent. Can it not be said, that in close to a period of three hundred years, modern North American culture has made homeless many of the trees and animals, insects and plants, spirits and people that once called this place home?

In saying all of this, I include myself as a contemporary American who has mostly lost track of his own roots. I do not wish to cast aspersions – that would be yet one more divisive shadow move, to be sure. The point in illustrating all this is to show the slippery way that shadow can elude awareness, how it gets projected in ways that call for a diligent exploration for seeing how these energies might show up and have been misplaced. This is a shadow perspective being carved in the interest of relearning how to be "at home" in our own bodies, for honoring the Indigenous Soul in each of us and in the world. The antidote to the displacement that many former Europeans, now called Americans, bring with us to this land could be to honestly seek to face all the shadow we've left behind us in our age-long exodus. The opportunity here is also to create an opening for ways to craft new yet original (of the origins) ways of being that honor everyone's dignity.

The way we relate to our shadows has deeply important ramifications for life. The only place to start, in a very real sense, is "at home". True shadow work involves apprenticing ourselves to the shadows we cast ourselves, which may be more fully recognized when we ponder the effect of their placements – be they on the earth below us or on our fellow living creatures we share this incredible, thirsty, thriving, hungry world with.

Anyone who has been in or is part of a committed relationship or marriage can know how the shadow comes out at the least convenient of times and oh-so-easily. We may look for and find these shades outside our selves in the world in many tones, yet we don't have to look far to see our relation to these unlived and unacknowledged energies. Many a rough nights sleep under cozy but not-so-tender circumstances on the couch could attest to this. Whether or not we bring more consciousness and ability for change to the table, we are perhaps indebted to see how the shadow shows up in the reflections that come floating back in intimate engagements with friends, lovers and family.

> Jung's statement below speaks to all this quite concisely, "Just as we tend to assume that the world is as we see it, we naively suppose that people are as we imagine them to be... Although the possibility of gross deception is infinitely greater here than in our perception of the physical world, we all still go on naively projecting our own psychology into our fellow human beings. In this way everyone creates for himself a series of more or less imaginary relationships based essentially on projection."[5]

In service of this conversation, and towards the trust of learning something worth acting upon, we might also consider that, if we can't or won't work with shadow energy where it appears in the mundane and everyday circumstances of our lives, we certainly won't be able to helpfully effect life as it exists for others in faraway locales. As already alluded to, one of the greatest shadow temptations is to distract ourselves from the way shadow influences our individual movements and relations by seeking to "save the planet". How many of us have gotten lost on the road of good intentions, in a shared improvement project, and chosen not to tend our own gardens? It may be easier to try to convince another to change than to face that task in our own lives. What then, are we to do to seek to avoid this unhelpful pitfall and to seek to lend a helpful hand towards effective change and tending a natural belonging in the world?

WORKING WITH SHADOW IN EVERYDAY LIFE

Along with seeking to identify the shadow in our dreams, we may also maintain a discipline for noticing when we become troubled by events, and people, in waking life. Often, we can locate a shadow connection when paying attention to both our dreams and the everyday trials we move through. When we identify such energies within and without, it is then that we might do something helpful about the way these energies play out in our lives. Owning the unsavory sides of our selves has the effect of discharging unbridled and un-useful destructive outcomes.

To give an illustration, let's say that I become aware of some jealousy about the success of a colleague. By allowing myself to see and feel that desire to have what they have puts me on notice that I am somehow being passive about my own deep longings and gifts. The knowledge of my envy poses me with the necessity for asking if I will seek to attain and give out what it is that I am jealous of. I now have a choice to make about acting on my own behalf and I may recognize that my feelings about the other person, my colleague, and their situation, require me to take responsibility for how I choose to live and to meet my capabilities for expressing my own gifts.

According to a Jungian approach, a good rule of thumb is to note how emotional we tend to get in the face of daily interactions. As we've noted, just because it's a projection doesn't mean that it isn't true. When something or someone troubles us, and we feel the need to justify our own actions and views, it's likely that the shadow is involved. This doesn't mean that we ought to seek to avoid the emotion or the shadow, rather, that they both bear a purpose for our lives.

There is an overlay of this phenomenon in our dreams that can serve as a form of grounded fleshing out about this notion. Often, we dream of people that outright disgust us, while at other times people appear in our dreams that we find irksome for various reasons. Primarily, I would say we don't dream of such folks so that we can set them straight in waking life! It's amazing how easy it can be to presuppose that when these people appear in our dreams, it's because the dreams are trying to tip us off to what's wrong with "Them" – and, by extension, what's right about "Us". This is not to say that such messages and occurrences don't also take place. This is one area where dream work, and life, can get tricky, for we do dream of others and sometimes for others, especially in a culture where so many people think that dreams are worthless bits of nonsense.

A reliable indicator for determining if the dreams are telling us to be on the lookout for others in waking life has to do with how true to waking reality the dream sequences and people seem to be in the dreams themselves. If the dream plays out like a scene that appears exactly like it could in waking life, then it *may* mean that the dream is forecasting a potential future event involving other people. The more surreal and dream-like the dream, the more *likely* that the dream is speaking to these energies as they exist within us. In all dreams, in my experience, the symbols and images, even if they appear to be literal are *also* still symbolic and speak to the dreamer about her or his own being and also often depict 'others' and their situations as well. The boundaries tend to get blurry at times. There are no "hard and fast" rules in this work, so it's helpful to ask questions of our selves, and each other about what the dreams might mean. This is also a portion of why it's so crucial to pay attention to these energies, so we can seek discernment around them. Certainty is not guaranteed in dreams any more than it is in waking life. The more we work with our dreams, the more we can get a trustworthy feel for the way they speak to us personally and universally, albeit amid some clear archetypal, and hence, idiosyncratic, diverse and difficult to contain realities.

Even in dreams that "tell the future", when we dream of others, on some vital and important level, the dream is making use of all its wise faculties to show us what is true about us on the inner planes as well. Even when dreams help navigate outer circumstances, they are showing us how we are currently experiencing shadow relative to our own psychic wellbeing. And, they are always seeking to help us to understand that the outer and inner, self and other are not as separate as we tend to think they are.

Endnotes Chapter 3

[1] James Hollis, "Why Good People Do Bad Things, Understanding Our Darker Selves", 2007, Gotham Books, p. 30

[2] Jeremy Taylor, "The Wisdom of Your Dreams", 2009, Tarcher-Penguin, p.237

[3] Jeremy Taylor, "The Wisdom of Your Dreams", 2009, Tarcher-Penguin, p.236

[4] Meredith Sabini, Editor, "The Earth Has a Soul, C.G. Jung on Nature, Technology and Modern Life", 2008, North Atlantic Books, Berkeley CA, p.169

[5] Carl Jung, "General Aspects of Dream Psychology", *The Structure and Dynamics of the Psyche*, Collected Works 8, par. 507

CHAPTER 4

Mythic Embodiments, the Roots of Life's Projects

"Mythology is the textbook of the archetypes"
Carl Jung

Old cultures have originated folkloric patterns of experience through story for a very long time. We still involve ourselves with mythic tales today, yet we tend to relate to them according to our literalized world-views. The old stories may still become trustworthy treasure chests for holding the eternal truths of our natures amid Great Nature's nature. Stories also fling the lid open so that the treasure can become ordinary everyday food. Myths resonate with us, because they accurately vocalize the dreamlike, true qualities of deeper paths. They help us remember and put back together, the realms within and beyond. Great stories also describe the directly observable physical world.

In his fascinating book *Tracking the Gods*, Hollis says, "… a greater intimacy with myth provides a vital linkage with meaning, the absence of which is so often behind the private and collective neuroses of our time… the study of myth is the search for that which connects us most deeply with our own nature and our place in the cosmos. Surely no more central issue confronts us collectively and individually."[1]

I would further suggest that myth equally offers an opening to valence between "our nature" and the cosmos such that the living personality of what seems to lie outside can be fully related with as well.

In Greek and Roman myths the god known as Eros, Amor or Cupid creates relationship between the divine and human through the impulsive, exacting and impassioned loosening of his arrows. We moderns have sadly softened and "cutified" Cupid to the extent that it may be easier to call this divinity by his less beleaguered monikers, Eros or Amor. Eros still holds some amount of dignity as a word in our time, though we often use this term thinking that it mainly refers to sensual and sexual action between lovers. The archetypal resonance of Eros includes yet stretches far past the limits of purely physical encounter into a fully relational and multiple-layered context of belonging and meaning that also involves spirit and soul.

As Michael Meade, Storyteller and Mythologist says, with the great stories it's not about whether the tale is true or false, right or wrong, made up or reflective of literal events. He says it's about finding orientation, about whether one is and ought to go "right or left... up or down?" The major function of myths is not distinctly historical. Rather, myths, fairy tales and folk stories provide a sense of inward and outward direction, serving up meaning that brings much value to our lives, which inherently exists within the cosmos. These fabrics of timeless tales find their origin within our very souls, in the deep designs woven there and also in the soul of the world. Stories describe kinds of ostensible falsehoods in fantastical form, in order to uncover the truth hidden inside our own spirits, souls, hearts, bodies and minds. *Our dreams do this all the time as well.*

It has often been noted that visionary consciousness forms the bedrock of mythic understanding and the arts via the narratives that get handed down, spoken, sung and written, across generations. Marie-Louise von Franz, a well-known authority on fairy tales, states,

> "I think it likely that the most frequent way in which archetypal stories originate is through individual experiences of an invasion by some unconscious content, either in a dream or in a waking hallucination... numinous experience is always talked about and becomes amplified

by any other existing folklore which will fit in. Thus it develops…"[2]

Fairy tales and mythology can be seen as *dreaming stories* that get passed on, because they involve the teller and the listener in vibrant parabolas that have the capacity to reveal wisdom sources to those who would attend to their many currents.

ARROWS AND SLINGS, OUR BLESSED PROJECTS

The story of Psyche and Eros, which first appeared in written form with ancient Greek writer Apuleius' *The Golden Ass* is no exception. When Venus, who recognizes herself to be the most beautiful and beloved of divinities, hears tell of Psyche's developing reputation among mere mortals as one more lovely than the Goddess herself, she sends her son Eros to Earth to teach Psyche a lesson and "put her in her place". Venus charges her own progeny to humble Psyche and ruin her beauty so that mortal people will remember to pay Venus her due, as Divine Feminine Beauty, and return to making offerings at the Goddesses' temples. The Goddess requires that Eros cause Psyche to fall in love with the most horrible and ugly man he can find in order to achieve this.

Eros accepts his mother's marching orders. Yet when he sets eyes on Psyche, such is her allure, that he falls in love with her himself and lets loose one of his bespelled sacred arrows. This act sets an entire initiatory adventure into motion in which Psyche faces many trials. Thereby, Eros too becomes more involved with the human realm through his love affair with a mortal woman, confronting and suffering his own tribulations along the way.

How like projection this is! We head off in life with some task in mind, possibly following the outer authoritative directive of someone we deem more powerful than our selves, only to upset the apple cart through an unavoidable rebellious act of the souls' deeper passions. One of the many lessons of this tale is not only that a male god and a female woman fall in love. The myth also suggests that when we humans gain favor in life and attract the attentions of divine forces, an encounter will ensue and the personality will be made to reckon with the larger energies of the eternal characters and persons existing as part of the cosmic order and in the soul. The human and the divine will find one another eventually, and inevitably come into relationship, "by hook or by crook".

Eros' projectile and Psyche's charm create the connection of spiritual and erotic intimacy between them, enmeshing the divine and the human. This story rings out across time and has been told and retold because it evokes a deeper truth about our own lives. This type of knowledge requires that we each contain, and have to learn how to live with, our all-too-human energies as well as those of the divine archetypes, the Gods and Goddesses, as they exist within our own well-crafted lives, dreams, great stories and everyday encounters.

Psyche is an ancient Greek word meaning both *soul* and *butterfly*. It is also a word used in connection with Carl Jung's notion of the Anima. Anima is Latin for "soul". This is the name he gives for the Soul Guide, the inner woman who can be understood, on one level, to *animate* physical matter and reality and which can be seen in a wild form in the many *animals* of the land as well as those in the sky, within the waters. Von Franz states that anima is neither purely physical nor completely spiritual, that her task is to embody and represent what is in between both, yet which is also very real. The anima, then, is a mediatrix of the in between realms of matter and spirit.

In the story of Psyche and Eros, we find an action of *animation* taking place, where the spirit of relating, embodied in the divine person of Eros, seeks to join with an earthbound soul, personified by the grounded yet somehow decidedly numinous human woman Psyche. This doesn't exactly make Psyche the anima of the story, per se. What it does mean is that this force, this Soul Guide or consort is somehow present and suggested by her person. In my wide viewing of many people's dreams, it's evident that such a mediatrix-consort appears at various times in various ways in the dreams of both men *and* women.

One of the main reasons mythologies, dreams and folktales survive throughout time is that they express vital teachings in multi-contextual forms that speak on important psycho-spiritual though equally practical, grounded levels. For, ultimately, soul and spirit as well as physis (physicality) can all be seen to be of great import to human, earthly life and death. Stories like *Psyche and Eros*, embody abstract ideas and give rise to blood-filled meanings, so that we may understand complicated forms of knowledge in a delicious, imaginative and relational manner. Stories such as this one help us to see where we ourselves are living, within the great dreams of a lifetime. The *story has us*, the *dream has us*, not the other way around, it turns out.

In describing what she terms "feminine consciousness", which is present within each one of us, woman and man, Marion Woodman evokes the powerful symbolic quality of a light refracting, which hints even further towards this numinous essence,

> "… like a prism… many-faceted, every facet being a mirror of the center, the center being in every facet."[3]

The great stories, small or big, affect us like our dreams do. Whether we remember or reflect upon them or not, they carry out and depict crucial, stylistically vivid, deeply descriptive questions and truths that help us learn how to live, and live how to learn, so that we might understand our selves, one another and our experiences while also helping us to carve out a place within our intelligence for the mysteries that move us, yet which may never be completely solved.

These movements of psychic reality can be felt as radiating out of a vibrant living center. They show how we might or might not take action in relation to who we seem to be and are becoming as well as how we might feel an actual, rooted sense of belonging to our little corners of the world. The more we seek to honor the dreams and stories that resonate with us on so many levels, going under, around and into them, the more we stand to gain from their vibrant, timeless energies.

In the story of Psyche and Eros, we witness the comi-tragic and serious reality of the way projections surprise and overtake us. The cloaked, not-yet-speech-ripe feelings in our hearts and souls draw us into adventures that show us what we didn't yet know about who we are and also the poignant, necessary tangled heart-strings of the divine commingling with the human. This revelation extends to the soils, creatures, elements and other threads in the

fabric that make up the wondrous garment of the cosmos of which
we too are sewn. These allegedly separate forces must find a way
into known relationship with one another, according to the dramas
that play out in our dreams, folk myths and fairy stories. The
divine seems to accidentally fall in love with the human and vice
versa in Psyche's tale; yet it may be no accident.

It's crucial to notice that projections bring us into
relationship with one another, as well as the divine. It seems such
projects cause us a bit of trouble. The projects of our lives also
enliven, inform and involve us in the great on-going endeavor of
belonging. So, it's helpful to choose to view projection itself as a
phenomenon that also aids and assists us.

Taylor sheds light on this with his well-wrought words,
"It is through projection that we usually gain the first
conscious, clear (though mistakenly attributed) glimpses of
currently unconscious aspects of our own being that are
pressing and clamoring for more conscious
acknowledgement, recognition, and expression in our
waking lives."[4]

There is a sense of destiny in the way that Eros and Psyche
come together in the ancient story as a consequence of this impulse

towards realizing unexpressed aspects of their beings. So too, we experience a sense of inevitability around the way we entangle ourselves in relationship with life's energies, the sacred, the natural world and one another through our need to become conscious of what we didn't previously know by projecting what is within us 'out there' onto others. This is all a kind of learning, really. It may be the 'only show in town' at the end of the day.

Similar energies exists in a likely lesser-known story that hails from a much different part of the world. The people who have cared for and kept this story alive have survived and lived with great allure and cunning in what can be considered a much more demanding portion of the earth.

Something vital within the story that follows in the next chapter has grabbed my imagination and invokes the many resonating onion-layers of human soul psychology and timeless spiritual themes pertinent to our day. Perhaps more so than the ancient tale of Psyche and Eros, the drama known as *Skeleton Woman*, may remind us of the inclusive motifs and realities of animals and elements, amid the apparently severe conditions of the lands where the Inuit people still live today. In this clearly aboriginal story, we may locate some of the struggles with which our own age is grappling. It is within such a framework, wherein we currently co-exist with so many others, that we can perceive an

insistent pulling on our sleeves, asking us to put back together
again the many pieces of the puzzle of "life on Earth" and to really
remember.

     If it is true that we are living in times of trouble, then let us
"run towards the roar" and find some helpful mischief in the North.
Let's go on a vision hunt, and knowingly enter this old yet
somehow timeless tale. We do so together but at a distance, with
an eye for life-carrying and death-laden foamy cold waves, the
swooshing wisp of well-brined seal whiskers, wildly related to
expertly handmade boats, sharpened and refashioned fish-hooks
and sparking, well-used flints. May we be willing to confront what
has been lost and what may yet be found on our shared yet
individual journeys.

Endnotes Chapter 4

1 James Hollis, "Tracking the Gods", 1995, Inner City Books, Toronto, Canada, p.8

2 Marie-Louise von Franz, "The Interpretation of Fairy Tales, revised edition", 1996, Shambala Publications, Boston & London, p.24

3 Marion Woodman, "The Pregnant Virgin", 1985, Inner City Books, Toronto Canada, p.170

4 Jeremy Taylor, "The Wisdom of Your Dreams", Tarcher/Penguin, New York, 2009, p.233

CHAPTER 5

Skeleton Woman

"For nothing can be sole or whole that has not first been rent!"
William Butler Yeats

In a time out of time, but also before our time and yet quite like the time we live in today, there lived a father who grew disappointed with his daughter. She had done something that nobody fully understood then or knows about now, which the father claimed caused him to throw his very own progeny over the cliffs into the sea. And that is exactly what he did; he dragged her off to the high cliffs near their village and tossed her into the icy ocean below.

As she sank down beneath those piercing waves, the fish and creatures there tore the bountiful flesh from her and fed until there was nothing left but bones. Among the watery depths, she existed as a forgotten memory of her former self and was buffeted about, rolling along within the tidal heave alongside crustaceans who traveled slowly and ploddingly across the ocean floor.

After many sunsets and day breaks and beneath the ever-changing silvery faces of the circling of the moon, the local fishermen eventually came to call this particular place, where the daughter had fallen, haunted as a result of the strange goings on that occurred whenever anybody went to do their fishing in that cove.

One day a lone man, who had strayed afield from his usual bearings, was out for his daily sea-hunt and decided to give his luck a whirl in those very ghost story filled waters. This fisherman seemed not to have heard that this part of the land and sea had come to be inhabited by troublesome spirits.

Because no other fisherman were to be seen, this man's hopes for a bountiful catch with which to feed himself and his kinsfolk filled him with an enthusiasm that sent him on his way, carrying thoughts of how pleased everyone would be with his haul if he could manage to fill his lines. With that thought in mind, he put out on the waves and began to cast his hook down in to the choppy, entrancing waters, feeling that he would surely find some big fish beneath the swells that lapped up against his tiny craft.

It wasn't long until he felt his pole set firm. At that instant he muscled in what his practiced body felt to be a mighty fish. For the weight at the other end of his stick tipped the gunnels of his sturdy kayak. Down below, the weathered and salt-soaked skeleton of a woman, that former little daughter, rose up under the tow of the fisherman's strength and determination. The barbs of his hook had lodged in the woman's rib cage and as she struggled to break free and fought being captured in this way, she sent the sea into a churning swirl about her while also tangling herself up in the fisherman's sturdy tackle.

He heaved and hauled to the point where he knew his catch was just below the surface and, turning for to bring the magnificent creature aboard, he didn't yet notice that he had actually caught a skeleton woman whose open places were filled with things of the deep sea growing inside her eye sockets and barely moving jaw. As he pulled his catch in she became totteringly snagged over the rimmed edge of the vessel. He turned with his own eyes wide and saw her there, propped by the jagged edges of her sharp, long and narrow teeth on the side of the boat. This vision sent his heart awhirl and to racing so that he nearly toppled over into the freezing waters himself.

The fisherman let out a shriek, "Aiiee!" But it was too late and his heartbeat drove him, heatedly and without a thought, to begin making for the safety of solid ground and the village. So convinced was he that the thing upon his boat was alive and chasing after him, he sought to flee for the enclosure of his ice-hewn hut. In this rush of excitement, and due to the thrashing waves and the breezing winds and her having gotten tangled as she had, the skeleton woman bounced and clattered the rest of the way into the little kayak… "Kerpluckity lump, kerpluckity bump…"

This ruckus gave the further impression that the skeleton woman was running and dancing after the fisherman himself, which only had the effect of increasing his fervor to return to shore.

Once he set foot upon the beach, the fisherman acted very quickly and if you saw him, you would say the poor man was barely able to breathe. He grabbed his fishing tackle as if by sheer impulsive habit and ran, skittering across the beach. His gear had become ensnared in the skeleton woman's bones in such a way that she could do naught but follow. As she did, she clacked, danced and bumped along giving the full impression that it was her intention to catch up the fisherman, whose only purpose had focused into the single desire to return to his humble dwelling.

Across hardened sand, ice and tundra he went. Passing over mossy rocks and crystallized watery edges, past the drying meat of other fisher folk, he aimed himself like a trusty spear homeward. The skeleton woman on his heels grabbed at pieces of fish drying in the wan northern sun, for so long had it been since she had fed herself in the way that suited her best, on the human food prepared in the way of her people.

The fisherman continued until he arrived to the portal of his igloo and dove in, unwittingly pulling his fishing line and the animated pile of bones with him. Once there, he had nothing more to do but stare across the room, shaking and shivering while the skeleton woman sat in a heap of misarranged bones opposite him. He lit a whale-oil lamp and began to calm himself somewhat and also found, after a while, that his heart began to fill with a certain warmth of kindness towards the skeleton woman who had followed him, as the firing of the lamp and the womb of his home added a much needed glow to his own rankled body and her bare, sea-washed form.

While gazing upon her, he oiled his fishing stick while also winding and untangling his gear. As he did so, he began to hum and then to sing a rhythm. "Oh na na, oh na na, oh na na". She herself kept quiet, feeling somehow that if she uttered a sound, the man might take her out and dash what was left of her on the stony rocks next to the ocean.

Maybe it was the familiarity of his cozy abode, and maybe it was due to the lighted lamp he had sparked up and its accompanying heat of licking flames and flickering light, and perhaps it was the percussive tune that had arisen within him, or some combination of all of the above and something more, but he felt a kind of grief-soaked sorrow for this skeleton woman who sat across from him now. As he intoned the little tune, he soon found himself rearranging and straightening up the skeleton woman's wave-worn frame. He fingered a flint from his cuff pocket and cut apiece a strand of his own hair to start a central fire in the hearth.

He remembered her as best he could in the way a human woman's bones ought to go. Until, at last exhausted by his adventure, he settled down and fell asleep under some animal skin blankets, awash in the communal dance of the now roaring flames of the hearth.

As the fisherman eased down into the melting embrace of his slumber, he began to dream the mysterious kinds of dreams that have been known to produce tears upon the cheeks of many a sleeper. Skeleton woman sat across from him and watched as the man dozed and dreamt. She witnessed a single tear as it squeezed out of his dreaming eye, where it trailed a glistening path down a wind-chaffed cheek. She realized at this moment how very, very thirsty she was. There, in the fiery glow of the ice hut, she leaned over and began to drink the fisherman's tears, and in this way sought to slake her ancient thirst.

Feeling partially revived with the liquid of this man's somnolent grief-bound vision, skeleton woman began to sing her own song and she also pulled the sleeping fisherman's heart from his breast with her bony slender fingers, beating it like a drum on both sides, "Da-boom-boom, Da-boom-boom-ta". As the percussive pulse softly and slowly surged, she began to sing the words, "Flesh, flesh... Flesh, flesh, flesh." As she sang and drummed on the heart and drank the too-long held back tears and the fuel of that fire crackled and popped, skeleton woman sang the very form of her body, slowly, fibrously, miraculously back into life upon the wizened frame of her rattled, salt-soaked and tattered bones.

In this way, it was only a matter of time before she had completely re-formed a body for herself, singing her lower regions back into life - thighs upon her desirously curved leg bones, breasts and heart upon and within her longing-drenched rib cage, able, knowledgeable hands and fingers, stabilizing, yet delicately robust toes and feet, her now glowing ocean-washed face, dark, soft, intelligent, yet well-lit and fire-warmed tender and fine hair, fierce, strong, wizened and beautifully arched backside, powerful furnace-womb of the belly, proud for nourishment and a properly attuned ear for digestive capacities, all these things and more that a woman needs to be whole within and without.

She continued to sing her enchantment, and as she did, the clothes came off the fisherman as he slept, until he was naked beneath the skins and furs, as she was, so that she slid under the blankets and next to his body there in the increasing heat and aura of belonging now taking place in the simple hut.

She carefully placed his heart back in the cave of his chest. They came close in this manner, skin upon skin, and awoke together in a now well recalled and beautiful way and created a life with one another as partners from that moment forward.

To this day, the people talk of skeleton woman and the fisherman who survived and thrived well ever after on the creatures from down below the surging ocean's surface, which the skeleton woman knew so deeply from her time beneath the icy waters and which the fisherman was learning more about with each passing day and night.

If you listen, you can still hear them out near the coast, singing their throaty songs of longing, grief and provenance, as their hearts and souls soar out upon the shifting winds that float above the ocean tides, or at least that's what the old ones say, and if the old ones don't know, then who does?

Me, I'm just here sitting next to the fireplace in the deep green redwood forest, singing and searching with you, casting my fishing line beneath the waters of ancient memory, in search of some songs and some catch that might help to feed us and more so, the old stories and the wild denizens of the ocean, the skies and the land, as we go through the many days and nights of our very own travels within this dream we call the Road of Birth, Life and Death.

CHAPTER 6

Sifting Among the Bones,
Learning to Feed and Be Fed by the Holy in Nature

"Well might a person in those days say there is a Dream that dreams us."
John Moriarty

As we gaze into the multi-faceted jewel of the story of Skeleton Woman, we see many dream-like qualities alive within in its genius tapestries. In fairy and folk tales, archetypal, transpersonal and universal energy patterns describing psycho-spiritual and other layers of existence are readily discernable through reading and telling as well as in hearing the tales. Such energies reveal an accompanying symbolic resonance of profoundly practical import, amid deep study and attention.

Taylor hints at this in his vastly imaginative book on "exploring universal themes in myths, dreams and the symbolism of waking life", *The Living Labyrinth,*

"A deeper conscious encounter with dreams and myths can nurture creative imagination, creative self-realization and expression, compassion, and courage in ways that no other effort of attention can achieve; and these are, as they have always been, the qualities and energies we need to confront and transform our eternal human predicament."[1]

I'd like to emphasize the import of approaching this story with a hearty amount of respect for the symbolic.

Shaw gives us this glowing light of understanding in his *A Branch from the Lightning Tree, Ecstatic Myth and the Grace in Wildness*,

"Within the realm of story a sign denotes, a symbol connotes. When images from the unconscious or myth are seen only as signs, they are robbed of their transformative power; their use as psychic guides is erased. It can only point towards a breakdown of the imagination when we interpret symbols as a sign... Mythic understanding is subterranean; it lives underneath. A woman who is really a seal, a Dragon obese with conquest, a bridge that is a razored sword – it is rash to suggest these doorways are falsehoods; they provide a poetic space for the imagination to flood into."[2]

Both Taylor and Shaw place importance on the living quality of stories, myths and dreams. When contemplating any story, as with any dream, it's crucial not to squeeze the life's blood from it in how we come to the exploration of helpful meanings.

Skeleton woman is a story that Clarissa Pinkola Estes has wondrously retold in her *Women Who Run With the Wolves*. Estes carries forth a profound poetry in relation to the way she offers her insights around and within the life of the psyche and mythology. This tale was shared with her by Mary Uukalat, and is an Inuit tale, which bears many similarities to the folk myths of Sedna.

It has been said that folk stories, in their deceptive simplicity, are less bound by the distinguishing mores of particular cultures than actual mythologies are, and hence may provide a rich portal for finding shared elements appearing in our dreams and waking lives and in Wild Nature itself.

In my experience, stories such as this one, which bear characteristics that belong to distinctly important, wise, complicated and beautiful cultures as well as earthly terrains, do also contain a healthy strata of evocative interwoven imaginal experiences, metaphors and symbols, which can speak to many of us, across time and space. A portion of the wound that most modern peoples have suffered through the devaluing of dream-sharing, as well as attending to mythic lore, has to do with the potential loss of meaningful, guiding and wily stories such as this one. Folk myths like *Skeleton Woman* hold the vulnerability, strength, potency and wisdom to reveal what I'll call a 'native soul intelligence' that can surely arrive within and without as a profoundly powerful healing balm for the timeless and time-bound ills that ail us and our fellow travelers. These tales help us relate to what we might call the otherworlds. These worlds are a kind of mystery, for on the one hand they seem to exist somewhere and sometime else, and we can also see them unfolding in the daylit worlds that enclose our human daily awareness. As Shaw sees it, we actually live in the stories themselves. We can see how this is the case when we apprentice our minds and hearts to the stories and our dreams and locate our selves within them.

Although dissimilar, we all do bear some inevitable identity with an inherent core of belonging, what Martin Prechtel, another venerable and beloved storyteller calls "the Indigenous Soul". Whether we are willing to acknowledge it or not, we all come from and depend upon the earth, the sun and the moon, the planets, the grasses, the four-leggeds and so much more. Each of us has, somewhere in our blood-memories of seeded spiritual and physical identity, a living connection with people and spirits who at one time lived within and alongside the natural world, with great respect. These kindred ones, indeed, not only held such a respect but did so adeptly, beautifully and proudly, even if they also wonderfully failed, in myriad ways, in their attempts to craft a life within the web of this wild world. If this weren't true, none of us would be here today. I don't think we honor that enough.

Many of us have forgotten this, or have willingly chosen to try to erase our mythic inheritances, usually in the pursuit of a more secure and comfort-bound occupation. As I see things, it is this quest for 'the ultimate insurance policy' that now has us in such a dire state as regards the very real hazards of global climate change and cultural collapse. I have retold this story, in the trust that it might reawaken the wily Soul of Nature within each of us who can find our place inside the tale. Here lies an alive, guiding symbolic intelligence and feeling tone that may instruct our visibly imperiled lives, postponed deaths and the cultures we co-create. In this seemingly simple story we could find a possible route of return towards the Nature of our natures and the viable living peopled fibers of soul, wood, mineral, water, air and fire who lovingly and continuously ask us to remember and care for them in return for all they give to us.

FINDING LOVE AND LIVING GRIEF
IN THE CLIMATES OF CHANGE AMID CHANGES OF
CLIMATE AND THE DEEP WOUNDS OF THE SOUL

Re-entering the story with an alert ear, an attentive eye, a furry-clawed paw and a wildly woven heart aimed towards learning, experience and meaning, we note that the tale suggests potent levels of resonance with contemporary and eternal human dilemmas to be found sewed into the ever-present wombs and tombs of Great Nature, wherein we ourselves reside. These inheritances betoken timeworn obstacles of the search for sustenance, love, relatedness, soul making and companionship. Something in the story speaks to the escalating challenges we are faced with by the now long purported ecological crisis. These days the buzz phrase is "climate change". We may think these two apparent directions in the story - love, intimacy, soul-searching and cultural/planetary crisis- are wholly set apart. Yet I believe this folk dream shows us that they may not be, after all is said and done. Such quests for rekindling a true sense of belonging will be seen to involve the loving, at times communal, living energies of the soul, bridging together an engagement with our deepest spiritual natures and those of our many diverse neighbors too.

Just as physical space and matter appear to inhabit certain tendencies and natural laws, so it appears to be the case with the psychic landscape, the territory of myths, folk tales and dreams. There are forms of order (and disorder!) inherent in these domains.

At the very outset, the trouble is announced, as it has been in many a dream and fairy tale. The father, we could say the masculine authoritative energies, for reasons that we may suppose are deliberately left unclear, dashes the youthful feminine, his own daughter into the ocean depths below the cliffs. The ocean's presence heaves forth here as the mysterious place of a distinctly different kind of life than we are accustomed to on dry land as two-legged humans.

The ocean is folk myth code for the Underworld. In many cosmologies, including the highly rationalized scientific mythology of our day, it has been said that we ourselves, at one point in our lengthy evolution upon the gods and goddesses green earth, crawled from those surging liquid-filled depths to find a life here upon the capacious and frequently forgiving land.

Perhaps this accounts for the lack of specifics around the fathers' impetus for tossing his daughter to a watery exile beneath the waves. From one view, this wounding in the story is a depiction of the masculine forces rending womanly youthfulness asunder. This perspective, I think, has much to say to us. It certainly looks a lot like the way that many men have mistreated many women and for quite some time now, through violence, objectification and an overall attempt to force feminine energies and people onto a lower level. Maybe, also, this is the attempt to avoid, throw away or devalue the woman *within* the man. We recall Shaw's words about the subterranean nature of myth here as well, the quality of an underneath, an unconscious underworld.

From a slightly different angle, it could be said that what we are witnessing here is the masculine's misguided, split, imbalanced attempt to rid itself of the energies of its own confusing and troublesome opposite. In Jungian parlance, we might say that here the masculine attempts to cordon itself off from the feminine energies by casting them back into the realm of the unconscious in an effort to keep the "safe" and the "risky" apart.

The fact that the young daughter is a member of the upcoming generation is an important detail. In this particular of the story we can see how the more established energy – which may itself be in need of restoration – can be reckoned as threatened by the growing and youthful side of the feminine which it is closely related to. Perhaps a part of the reason the male powers seek to be rid of these energies has to do with an incitement to maturation, grief and renewal. After a lifetime spent developing an established personality, it can be tempting to settle for the well-polished status quo.

In the ho-hum, everyday world, we see this kind of refusal to admit the youthful and womanly energies in our actual downfalls. The ideals of young women are pushed down or aside and left unconsidered for the supposedly more experienced and knowledgeable voices of conventional "progress" and mass techno-culture. In such a clime, there may be little support for newly sprouting principled desires to grow sustainable food, in beautiful olden time, life-giving ways, for example.

The so-called feminine feeling side, the receptive inner natures of young men are also shot down when cultural stereotypes resist the grief-soaked emotions and tears that are released through the voices of youthful poets, storytellers and musicians. Whole scores of new soldiers are once again sheared, shaved and lined up to suffer unexpected traumas in the strangely dubbed first worlds' on-going battles across the face of the blossoming and ever-dying, fecundating earth. It used to be a great measure of a true warrior that he (or she!) was able to cook and serve up great feeling through the rendition of song and poems and through great tales shared with many.

The depth of wisdom to be found in folk stories is no trifle. Although we might be tempted to think of the father as having murdered and killed his daughter, the story itself actually says no such thing, exactly. She *is* cast into the icy waters. In that living fluid, her memory-holding body is largely stripped of its humanity in the form of her flesh. Yet she continues to exist in a new realm of belonging as a bony being, which we can feel to be a kind of exile. Still and all, this is where the daughter, the young woman energy establishes a relationship with the very source of life and renewal as it is experienced to this day for people living along the many coastlines of the worlds oceans, in touch with the Indigenous Soul. When the flesh is eaten away, something that remembers and is uniquely necessary and ancient remains.

It's like Marion Woodman's words about how dreams are initiatory plunges, referred to by Shaw as

"… an underworld detected in dreams, a moment when we brush the wing-feathers of mortality, when we take a rough push into the nettles. Traditionally, it lives outside the walled city of the intellect, in the rough places, or underneath our feet, nearer the extremes of hot or cold."[3]

And from Woodman herself,
"The descent is a mythological term for the period during and after a powerful event in which the ego has been overwhelmed by a wave from the unconscious. Energy that is normally available to consciousness falls into the

unconscious. That is known as journeying to the underworld, a state in which the creative energies are going through transformations that the unaware ego may know nothing about."[4]

This being cast down into the waves of the icy ocean has much more about it than a straight depiction of the casting away of the womanly forces of youthful life. Yet this opening act also clearly relates a level of actual damage too. It's as if something that has been held "on high" by the fatherly powers is in need of a lowering. This appears as a downward fall that has crucial learning embedded within it on many levels.

As Pinkola-Estes has it, Skeleton Woman is an archetypal personage of Lady Death Herself. We find a parallel in the Greek narrative of Persephone who is abducted by the God of the underworld, Hades. Through her own trials of going under and down, she becomes the wife of the underland ruler and a kind of mediatirx for the upper and lower worlds. Skeleton Woman is born from the symbolic 'death of the daughter'. The wily insight of the tale shines forth several truths about the way that what dies away doesn't disappear, rather it assumes a different form.

In a very palpable way, this tells us how the source of all the qualities that we might relate to as belonging to the feminine, somehow belong to and bring us back towards relationship with the mysterious living and dying that churns beneath the mighty waters of the oceanic realm. This is not only a place where the Waters of Life dwell, it's also a seemingly eternal well of the ancestors, the mysterious womb of the unknown memories that yet originate domains for the kind of forces that can feed life, out of the very real presence of symbolic and actual death. Perhaps this period of ocean exile holds a more profound meaning, that we may be likely to overlook, due to our contemporary assumption that anything painful, challenging and difficult must be "bad" or wrong.

> Estes says,
>
> "The Skeleton Woman who lies under the water is an inert form of deep instinctual life, which knows by heart the creating of Life, the creating of Death… Refusing to allow all the cycles of Life/Death/Life… causes the Skeleton Woman nature to be ripped from her psychic lodgings and drowned… Skeleton Woman is always thrown over a cliff when… we misapprehend the use of transformative cycles: when things must die and be replaced by others."[5]

One of the great effects of stories and dreams is that they render what we otherwise seek to understand abstractly. Stories give us a characterized, clearly reality-bound form that assumes a symbolic level at the same time it evokes actual truths, as they exist in the world around us. The symbolic and the actual are thusly interwoven.

I achingly agree with Shaw, who voices his distaste for the kind of language that utters such words as "feminine" and "masculine". He accurately raises our attention to the fact that these ways of describing observable and felt realities of real inner and outer people and energies are "bloodless". It's my impression that we are living in a time where we could begin to seek to create a more sanguine lingo. At times it's tricky to articulate what we might mean without use of such distinguishing words. In the interest of making an attempt, and in a poetic leap, therefore, let us refer to these energies as "the woman within" and "the man within" where it seems possible to do so. In various linguistic shades, let's seek to put some flesh on the very bones of the creatures that we ourselves may have flung over the cliff at one point in time in order to revision a wounded form of vibrancy in our own way of speaking about and relating to these people that we also are. Maybe then we will revivify energies and matters in the story here, but also in the ever-unfolding stories of our own lives as well as the lap of the world that gives us a place to call home.

HAUNTED AMID THE EVERDAY HUNT

Another way of carrying and living the story, allowing it to live through us, paradoxically yet wonderfully, would be to consider that the father energy sends the woman of the soul towards a *rite of passage*. She is forced to find herself in a low and watery domain that strips her to an essential core. This being torn down creates an accord with a much deeper nature, the ocean and the living creatures that sustain a more fluid, ancient stratus of heaving, liquid, dynamic and teeming existence. The story can be said to be offering an antidote that shows how the more authoritative energies have placed the inner woman and the daughtering powers in a place of tidal swells that we all may be answerable to.

If the tale of Skeleton Woman depicts a wound to the woman without and within, we'd also do well to reckon with the inherent meeting taking place here with the Life-Death-Life cycle. Who amongst us does not try to cast away the frightful goddess who confronts us with the knowledge that death is irrevocably the flip-side of life, the goal of its lengthy undertakings?

One of the biggest mistakes I have witnessed myself and others make, is to literalize the experience of death in dreams and stories. It's been said that Western culture is a "death-phobic" civilization. Somehow death is likely to be cut-off from the rest of life in our experience. The closer we look, and the more questions we ask about the way people not only talk and think about death in North America today, the more we might consider that death phobia is not too strong a phrase. It seems that part of the effect of the vast scientific air of modernity has also cordoned us off from the event of human birthing. Why haven't more of us been present at the births or deaths of family, friends and loved ones? Why aren't these great moments, the mighty bookends of our time here, something that we get to participate in? I think this is all connected to how we read and work with death in dreams and stories.

We need to ask such questions of ourselves, each other and of the culture in which we may find we are cut off from the most profound experiences that occur within a human lifetime. I have great respect for what Michael Meade imparts about death and dying, which may elucidate this,

"Modern mass cultures tend to overlook the uniqueness of individual souls while also avoiding the presence and meaning of death. Whereas traditional cultures would introduce the presence of death at the onset of life, modern societies put off questions of death until the very end. Even then, many refuse to admit the inevitability of death or the possibility that their death could be meaningful. Modern cultures are forgetful when it comes to the unique nature of each person and disoriented when it comes to the end of life."[6]

In a number of ways, our language about life and death bespells us; we could acknowledge this by assessing the value that we place on life over death. Consider all the means we use to attempt to prolong life, for the mere sake of living longer, as if that in itself was somehow an achievement that makes it worthwhile. We call our stint here as humans a "lifetime". Much of our language centers upon phrases like "quality of life" and evokes metaphors and supposed realities founded upon growth. Are we meant to grow forever? When and where do we also decay like leaves do in Autumn? Where does our thinking place the seasonal and mythic, cyclic energies of decline, dying and death? The ancient Greeks knew something about this. That's why they cast the underworld as such a real and important place. Almost any culture around the world that we could describe as pre-modern has attended to the realties of life *and* death, without excluding one for the other.

I was present during my own fathers' death, and can say without hesitation, that his dying time afforded myself, and my family a real and true sense of what death asks each of us. There's something truthful about acknowledging the inherent ceremony of death. One of my father's gifts to me was the actual willingness he showed towards honestly recognizing that he was about the business of dying and knowingly participating in it.

Dad had lung cancer caused by his work with asbestos. He chose not to go through chemo, an unpopular move near as I can tell, and he also wrestled consciously with the various symptoms he was engaged by leading up to his death by declining most of the pain medication he was prescribed. I'm not saying that there might not be times when chemo would be called for and when meds might also be helpful. I am saying that my father, whom I barely knew, was clearly involved in his own death and with his people during the moments that formed his own dying. He made it known to my self and my sister that some healing with us, and an honest movement through dying were more important to him than sheer comfort. His heartful choice to remain mostly free of the techno-medical establishment is living testament that a person can die well, with dignity amid the mess of a trying illness like cancer.

Within our own fragile collection of days and nights, there is much that we are asked to witness as dying away. From the rise and fall of each proud season in this challenging world, to the various psychological identities that we put on and take off like so much clothing hung upon the body, there are many aromas of seasonality revealed upon the paths we tread. I sense we might do well to distinguish between what we can know as *symbolic death* and *actual dying*, which may be related, yet also are likely much further apart than we like to think.

THE CENTER CAN'T HOLD, LIFE AND DEATH AT THE EDGES

Let's return to the story of Skeleton Woman. At the moment our hunter appears, it seems that there is more than a touch of the naïve about him. He heads off to catch food in a place that more experienced folk avoid . From our view, we're given the knowledge that this cove where he seeks nourishment is a ghostly locale – information respected by the fisher-folk of his kindred. The boldness of our lone fisherman is a tone that's needed in our lives today. His daring choice looks to be a willingness for entering the edge-territories that we could say confront us in various locales in our own daily rounds. We might intuit that our fisherman is a youthful representative of the man inside each one of us, as well as an echo of a kind of man we may find peopling the earthly world we inhabit. His spirited nature is perhaps not a superficial or literal "one-size-fits-all" variety. It can be felt and experienced as a soulfulness that bespeaks the qualities of an impassioned awareness – the kind of orientation that leads with heart and is able to learn rather than to simply know.

The haunted quality of these waters arises from the wounding that has taken place for so long around the dismembering of the woman of our souls - the actual women in our lives, yes - but also the woman within nature and within our very natures and the Woman of the Soul of the World.

Our fisherman's naivete is more like a much-needed willingness to risk than it is a flat-out ignorance. It betokens a lack of cynical avoidance. There doesn't appear to be any 'know-it-all' flavor in his style. Again, let's consider Marie-Louise von Franz's idea, where she has identified this character in myth and folk wisdom as the "Dummling",

> "Dummling represents the new conscious attitude which is capable of contacting the feminine... he is the one who is called stupid and seemingly unlucky. But if you look at his behavior more closely, you see that he is simply spontaneous and naïve; he takes things as they are... We

should always look at these stories as we do the dreams of individuals and ask what conscious situation is compensated by such a myth."[7]

Von Franz details, in much of her work on folk myths, and especially in connection with Dummling, how this innocent fool in stories comes out in response to the beleaguered and destructive King energy. Here the King would appear in our tale as the father who casts the daughter away at the very opening. The old attitude is often a prematurely closed one. The antidote to this appears in the willing and bumbling young masculine force who still has much to learn him self. This is a helpful and true force that connects the generations. We might learn a thing or two ourselves by attending to such spirits of spontaneity.

Coming at this from a symbolic angle, we see how it's possible for older, more experienced energies (and people!) to become stagnant. In the unwillingness to confront and risk both that which haunts and the ever-renewing youthful energies, the old ones may fail to become wise. Another way of saying this is that it's possible to grow into an *older* rather than into an *elder*. A mistake of growing old, especially in the modernized West, appears to be to seek ever and greater forms of certitude and safety, rather than recognizing the timeless wily energies of nature and the psyche. The staid choice to ignore and do away with the youths takes away from and wounds the coming generations, making life more difficult and despairing for the young but also for everyone else. This has to do with the boons in taking risks.

In this spectral air of the place alongside the sea lives the massive wounding that haunts our human ability to remember and care for what has been sacrificed, made sacred, in order to race ahead towards an imagined goal of supposedly well-insured and finalized security. Here lies the ghost of the all-too-human attempt to root out the soul qualities of being, belonging and essence, the young, new and unexpected energies of spirit and soul, existing in the fisherman and the disembodied, wounded daughter. The youthful woman and the risk-taking man exist within each of us, and in the spirited natural world as well.

In the modern world we have driven forward into one form of collapse after another. Cultural collapse and empire have torn the flesh from the very bones of the natural world, the indigenous cultures around the planet and continue to do so even now. We find ourselves in the midst of a much disputed, though clearly evident, enormous crisis within the vital matrix that surrounds and feeds us. Ebola, melting ice caps, imperiled polar bears and native cultures, disappearing and extinct plant and animal species, forgotten, endangered songs and languages, dances and ceremonial practices – all of these and more form the body of the flesh that has been eaten away from the daughters' bones. We witness this when we see the layers of her being that exist as The-Great-Woman-Who-Lives-Among-Us in the Ever-Spiraling Wilderness, in the swelling waters below, the cyclically falling and rising breath-filled land beneath our feet and the storm-spirit-filled skies above our heads.

On some important wavelength, we can all be alike to the hunter who wants to feed and nourish his family and himself. We must go into the haunted cove to find this nurturance. We may find ourselves there today or someday soon, surprised at what has been cast away by the supposedly more knowledgeable generations that have been in charge (with our complicity) up until now. Nature's nature requires that we face and live the grief of what gets cast away in an attempt to make life more secure. Such a response goes beyond recognizing these energies and events as feelings or emotions and the story shows us how the hunters' way of *enacting grief* comes out of his daily work, as a thing to be lived, not an inner state to be poked at or evaluated beneath a magnifying glass, or gotten over in a prescribed period of time.

What has been thrown away, which has died, is truly not gone. So the story tells us. It has actually been eaten away, altered and stripped to its eternal and instinctively memory-filled core.

Skeleton Woman is down there, remaking herself, being returned and reanimated by something and someone else, call it the Holy Divine in Nature if you like, to a heart of belonging and being. She fashions a part of the larger-than-life energies of the depth-inducing, teeming powers of the mighty oceans. Her being eaten is also a way that her life can be seen to feed both life and death. For a time, at least, her body becomes the cloak of the oceans' stirring enormity that surrounds her for miles and miles. It's equally no accident that the waters are frigid and exist in a place that is chilling to human sensibilities.

This aspect of the tale can be seen to describe the frozen potential of emotions and feelings, which may be warmed up to, lived out and might lead us to spirited, soulful engagements with all that is. The period of exile of the young daughter in the freezing waters is the story's expert way of revealing an attempt to assign the Woman of the Soul to a life "on ice".

IN EXTREMIS –
NATURE'S OPPOSITES AND THE CONIUNCTIO

"Enantiodromia" is an old Greek word for the balancing of energies in the psyche, the world and the cosmos. According to this old and very real phenomenon we may witness nightly in our dreams, all things will seek a native, so-called inner and outer balance. As a reflection of psychic realities and archetypal forces, what is frozen must eventually thaw out. The modern tendency to put certain feelings and ways of acting aside in favor of achievement is also prone to the balancing act of enantiodromia. It could be said that, in terms of emotion and feeling, people either tend towards one of the extremes of fire and/or ice, or attempt to avoid both in the lukewarm mediocrity of a seemingly safe middle. Many today seem to opt for the so-called neutral position.

For the Inuit, the cold and freezing natural world would, of course, be an ever-present part of everyday life. It's known that these folk have a myriad of words in their language simply to describe different kinds of snow, wind, sun and ice. The storied landscape of *Skeleton Woman* depicts an essential psychic struggle in terms that are understandable as they relate to the physical elements of the Inuit world. And yet there is also something perceivably shared across cultures about the experience of life's daughtering energies falling into frigid waters and the very natural experience of sensually felt temperate realities.

Even in places on the earth where freezing temperatures are not a reality, where temperatures are much higher, when certain conditions occur with the weather that include cooling, might people there have a sense of being cold? I recently asked a friend who grew up in Mexico about this. He said it was very hot in his childhood locale. When I inquired whether there were times that the people got cold, he said that when it rained, they definitely felt chilly. We compared this to the cold in Northern California where we both now live. He told me that where he lived 'south of the border', the people surely felt what cold was like, even though it was a "tropical" place. This relative "cold" is felt as a slowing down, a kind of physical stagnancy. In the tale, Skeleton Woman has been assigned to a lower place that is devoid of human warmth.

And yet, the ocean contains *salt* and we may therefore perceive that it will never completely freeze. Some 'fluiditas' is maintained even in the northern regions where freezing cold predominates. So too, our human grief must once more find its way to the surface to be heated, lived as an action. Real sorrow needs to be held where a 'salt-of-the-earth' style can prevent it from ever becoming totally constricted. There's paradox in the fact that the daughter has fallen into the very place that contains essential characteristics of the forces of nature that we ourselves must relate with in order to be whole. To live with fire and ice may be the making of a way that includes for the wounds that are a portion of any true 'whole' form of belonging. When we knowingly dwell within the extremes of nature, we may, perhaps cease to create false extremes that unnecessarily threaten the natural forces and beings whom we accompany on the journey.

The crustaceans, kelp, fish and other watery critters who fill in the vacant places where the young daughters organs and flesh once resided carry a vivid living-dying message too. When people disregard what's young and tender, gentle yet fierce, irrational but ensouled and are concerned largely with production versus essence, that which is cast out within our selves and in our world, like Skeleton Woman is in the story, cannot truly be eradicated. What dies comes back. So there's a reality of what's old and past that is key too. Tenacity, transformation, eternity and evolution (meant here as *unfolding*) are reflected in Her return from Death. We recall that the divine may flow through and seek to express itself through us. Remember Sudama and Krishna? But we would be wise not to identify with the divine, seeing ourselves as "It". Rather, we can know that we are surely human beings able to open our experience to the goddesses and gods of the mythic realms. For a time, as with the little daughter who was turned in to a Skeleton Woman, it may seem that we are subsumed by the sacred.

In first-hand accounts of shamanic initiations and vision quests, the person being called towards a rite of passage undergoes an imaginal, yet very real experience of having all the flesh torn from their spirit bodies. Stories from various cultures recount how one who is called goes down to the underworld and is ripped to pieces.

> Stephen Larsen, in his *The Mythic Imagination*, quotes, "The Tungus say, 'Before a man becomes a shaman he is sick for a long time. His understanding becomes confused. The shamanic ancestors of his clan come, hack him to bits, tear him apart, cut his flesh in pieces, drink his blood'".[8]

We can easily apply this to a woman who is called towards a shamanic initiation. There are women shamans, even in Siberia where the word itself originated and the healing art of shamanism is practiced to this day by both genders. There is clearly a shamanic-initiatory layer to the Skeleton Woman story.

Lest we feel that such an observation leads us too far astray from the Inuit backbone of the folk myth, let us also consider the following words from a classic authority on the subjects of initiation and shamanism, Mircea Elidae, related to cultures close with the Inuit,

> "The angakuts of the Iglulik eskimos are able in thought to strip their own bodies of flesh and blood and to

contemplate their own skeletons for long periods. I might add that visualizing one's own death at the hands of demons and final reduction to the state of a skeleton are favorite meditations in Indo-Tibetan and Mongolian Buddhism."[9]

To dismember someone or something is akin to 'unremembering', and can amount to a great forgetting and taking apart that invites a further experience of remembering – a putting back together. We see the way our young daughter is torn apart, taken down to the very memory of her living form and all the forms that gave form to her. This includes the Ancestors of every living thing, present in the salty oceanic mass, disintegrating sinew-laden bones, containing the marrow and the memory of the DNA, the biological, matter-bound memory of all those who have come before. This "separatio", to evoke an alchemical term, can be said to be like the manner in which things fall apart when we pretend to be able to bend life to our isolated human strategies. Every separatio hints at a balancing move towards coniunctio, or union.

THE LIFE-DEATH-LIFE CYCLE
IN WORLD AND PSYCHE

I live on and maintain a small vegetable and rabbit farm with my partner in the Northern California woods. Throughout the seasons, we see the Life-Death-Life dance in action, right outside, upon our doorstep and in our own home. I keep a writing trailer, an old 1940's Fireball camper, on the land. If this shelter is neglected for more than a few months, the natural energies of the forested wood begin to pull it back into the very earth from whence it once originated in its many component parts.

The aged but sturdy tires need to be checked and refilled periodically and have been slightly elevated up off the ground so they won't more quickly be devoured back into the hungry earth from which they were once wrought, hailing from trees in the rainforests of Central or South America I'd guess. The whole rest of the structure needs to be tended through ripping, springtime northwesterly gusts, pounding and insistent, sometimes gentle rains, and blistering summer into fall heat. During these moody shifts in terrestrial temperament, the forces of wind, rain, shadow and sun, those beings that some have called weather spirits and others gods and goddesses of this middle earth, find every crack and crevice through which it is possible to enter, stretch, peel, crack or otherwise rework, dismember and have their way with this arguably tough little hut on wheels.

The land and our house, as well as the garden and animals are prey to the same forces – all of which are also sustained through constant care and attention. As we cover, check, water, harvest, feed, dig, fertilize, watch, replant, warm up, cool down, dry out, pray for, sing to, dance alongside, speak to and listen for all the mighty forces of the forest and the nearby ocean, things are determinedly torn to shreds to be regrown once more. All this happens according to the deeply intelligent forces of the nature of Nature naturing amid this wondrous place. No matter what we do, some portion of life here must fall into the death jig wherein we are beseeched to help sing life back to life, and death unto dying. Every movement we make is, at best, an attempt to further synchronize with and learn from these powers of belonging, that necessarily include cycles of death-birth-death-birth. This amounts to and begins to look like a kind of maintenance of and for the Holy Divine in Nature, as we find it outside and within our own beings and resonating within all the pulsating life of the wilding forces about us.

Similar phenomena occur in our psyches, as well as throughout the fabric of our various human cultures. These powers live and die among myriad natural landscapes in which humans are invited to find a collaborative purpose of belonging to the world in which we all live and breathe. This earth is where we will also die amongst so many other living-dying-birthing beings.

Psychologically, we could speak of all the tending that the gardens of our many relationships require; these blood-ties exist with other people, and are woven into the living soils, plants, stars, animals, elements, trees, birds, skies, mountains, insects, fish and waters. Our gardens, literal and symbolic, can be a creative practice as well. As Miguel Unamuno said, "The only thing that lasts is the work turn to the work". How many of us have had the experience of not tending to our gardens only to realize one day, in our momentary forgetting to nourish, finding much to our chagrin and grief, that some tenderness and sweetness has been pulled apart due to our ignorance? Anyone who has experienced a break-up or divorce, suffered a rift of friendship, or watched an actual garden fail and falter may know what I'm talking about.

WHEN WE FORGET, SOMETHING ELSE RECALLS

Back in the Inuit story, our youthful daughter is carved down to an ossified frame. In places where the recognizable qualities of a formerly well-housed personality and thriving body once resided, other living energies that have a life in the dark watery depths rush in and take residency.

In this journey to the underworld of the sea, the daughter is wounded, to be sure, yet there is also a gift-like purpose that is bequeathed upon and within her. Taylor once more, in reference to the tale of Sedna and our shared identity in relation to the down-going directions, says:

> "All people who make the courageous choice to live more consciously, creatively and expressively must make a 'descent into the depths' to seek the creative ideas and energies that lie deep within."[10]

In our dreams, that which we have overlooked or not known to be careful towards, may show up as starving, wounded people and animals, as children who appear undernourished with flesh shrunken down to the bone. We ourselves may experience being torn apart at the hands of some vicious, hungry and powerful force while asleep in our beds. The good news is that by apprenticing ourselves to this inevitable pulling apart, we may identify the need to make offerings to what holds us up, like the very skeleton that holds up our own human bodies. We may allow our hearts and souls, as well as our minds to surrender to the deeper, wider and more powerful sources of life who inform us, just as they do with Skeleton Woman in the forever churning ocean waters.

One of the best offerings to make, is to give our attention, feelings and thoughts to the practice of carrying the stories of our dreams, our deaths and our lives. By recalling, sharing, thinking about, feeling and entering their imaginative deep waters, we show these vital beings of the otherworlds that we recognize the need to care for them.

ENTANGLEMENT

Our fisherman unwittingly connects with the lost form of the very thing that can be seen as most essential to our own contemporary lives. Through his innocent yet real willingness to seek nourishment in the haunted waters, he winds up recovering that which has been rent asunder, or was never fully known to the rest of us. It's no easy task, however, to re-member She-Who-Is-Able-To-Be-Refashioned-By-The-Living-Oceans. In doing so he must face his fears and the truth of what has been done to The Woman of the Soul, to the little daughter, to life, death and the living-dying earth as a result of this throwing away.

There he is, we can see him in his tiny well-made yet vulnerable vessel, out upon the waters, at the edge between what we're aware of and that which we aren't. The fisherman is like any of us who are invited to seek to establish a living dialogue with the cosmos and the inner reality of the psyche, as well as the living so-called ordinary world in which we all seek to make a life.

Let's pay heed, he is not out there seeking to feed and please himself, primarily, though as the story is told it's clear that our fisherman is also prone to the same uninitiated desires that many of us may also be known to give a home to. The hope exists in him that he might make a "big catch" that could last a long time, impress others and possibly make his life somehow easier and more successful and his work less strenuous.

At the same time, he is looking to find food for his people. He is hunting and doing what indigenous nature does in the setting of the wild, near to the village. In this detail of the story, I see that the young man is seeking to be *useful*. The story doesn't say so directly, yet if we reflect upon the tale in the context of Inuit culture, we at least have to admit that even if our fisherman is alone, his hunting is also for his clan. Maybe he suffers some of the desire to have what he catches all to himself; yet the story shows how he is given to realize through adventuresome suffering that he is not alone or isolated, and that there are others who need something from him – in this case, at least, the Skeleton Woman.

The story shows the need for an initiation into adulthood and usefulness in the life of this fisherman – and the rest of us, I would posit. In this caveat we find a revelation of the Indigenous Soul, which recognizes, in a way that our modern proclivity for rugged individualism seems to have overrun, how the food being sought is for all of life, not just for the individual.

Such understanding sees and feels the indebtedness that is created out of being fed. This quest extends beyond – but includes - the human need for sustenance. For, the Skeleton Woman our hunter entangles is no longer merely a human girl turned woman. She has been knitted up with the living forces of the very ocean and the underworld itself, and his catch consists of these living and nutritive energies who also need to be fed. We know as much because they have been feeding off the young daughter's humanness while she was in the oceanic realm.

There is also a beautiful and instructive weave in the tale that alerts us to the nature of projection. We often speak of the 'hooks' that we hang unknown energies upon. The fisherman goes hunting and his hook gets caught in the ghostly frame of a being whose nature is much different to what he thought he was out looking to encounter. In going for his "big catch" the fisherman gets way more than he has bargained for. Not only is his haul not simply fish, it's a deathly specter of a totally unexpected quality.

For Skeleton Woman's part, in her state of existing within the not-yet-speech-ripe, she is spontaneously 'caught' to the surface, all the while seeking to get free of the involving efforts of the naïve man who has hooked her. In the effort to break loose and avoid this resurfacing, she becomes entangled and her bones get all jumbled up.

These are classic telltale signs of projection in action! Any man or woman looking for a passionate encounter, friendship, love or nourishment can and does easily engage these dynamics. As von Franz puts it in a fairly psychologized language, speaking of the mythic *Return* which we are now witnessing in terms of the daughter's path back into the village as well as the fisherman's connection with Soul,

> "If one is caught in a projection that disturbs… whether it be an attraction that is full of fascination or hatred or obstinacy in clinging to a theory or an idea, at first one is carried along by a current of powerful affect as well as of desire or inner demand (to 'devour' the beloved object…)."[11]

Notice the relevancy of the kind of language that von Franz uses to describe the qualities of projection that parallel with our tale. The reality of being *caught, disturbed, clinging, being carried along on the current* and the energy of *devouring*. All these ingredients are present in our story. A desire to find some satisfaction along the well-trod paths of everyday life winds up turning into a surprising meeting with someone who can ultimately be experienced as much different than first envisioned. Skeleton Woman is caught up by the fisherman, he clings to her, and she to him, by hook, fear and gear. The little daughter turned Skeleton Woman is disturbed from her lonesome state by the fisherman and it's all the result of human desire to find and devour nourishment and that initial act of annihilation, whence the daughter is cast into the ocean by her father.

When we sincerely go hunting for sustenance we will encounter more than we first imagined we would. We sense that the fisherman is mostly unschooled. The young daughter is as if on a heroine's quest of initiation in the underworld. We see, once the story is under way, that Skeleton Woman is also really a divine personage, and in her being called to the surface, she is responding to the inner desires and willingness of the fisherman. We might also imagine that the young daughter in Skeleton Woman, and the very Goddess herself desire to be related with and that the daughter has truly become possessed. Despite all the thrashing, these wild women want to surface, devour and be fed. They also need to be teased apart and acknowledged in their rightful places. These details of the narrative describe how these energies of man/woman, human/divine, known/unknown attract one another and then it's as if "all hell breaks loose".

The fact that the fisherman reels in this human-divine creature of the sea, with her human frame still somehow intact tells us that it's not enough to catch some fish, go home, eat it and continue in the way that things have been, day after day. More wants to be revealed, and it's exciting that this is so! Something fearful and yet courageous has taken place. Some balance has been knocked out of place and is now returning to be re-aligned. The story shows that, even in the necessary daily work of seeking to feed and be fed there is a call to dealing with the obstacles that arise out of the mysterious waters of the seemingly ordinary places of our daily toil. The Great Adventure is part-and-parcel of the everyday pursuit towards feeding and being fed.

UNIO CORPORALIS, THE RETURN TO BEING HUMAN

When looking at the parable from the angle that sees the coming together of man and woman, we see that ideas which were held about "what was what" shifts rowdily within the engagement. As far as projection goes, here is a kind of unveiling of what lies underneath the supposed surface. When two or more people meet in any setting, we at first see reflections of who and how we believe and see each other to be, which is always relative to how we are ourselves. We give off certain tones of identity that we hope will be perceived and admired by the other. Eventually, the skeletons come out of the closet, and the whole range of emotions including a desire to run emerges. This is the churning of the waters by Skeleton Woman as much as it is the running homeward of the hunter.

Failures have a certain kind of humor within them. Courage is not the absence of fear or mistakes. The word itself comes from the "vulgar latin" for heart, *cor*. This is the pitch with which the fisherman meets the skeleton woman, though he appears to have no other choice once she's "hooked". He is willing to go through all the stages of getting close to his projected version of reality. He doesn't cut her loose, after all. He chose the haunted cove in the first place, despite its unpopularity. As he witnesses what he has brought up out of the watery depths, his trepidation overtakes him. Despite his very human response – of seeking to run to safety – she follows him right to the center of his own hearth, and *he brings her there*.

The "hearth" shines forth a quality of courage and heart. This place in any home is surely the center where a kind of rhythm is maintained without which life could not dance its way into the ever-turning spirals of many Life-Death-Life cycles.

The medicine in the story serves up the presence of this force of the shape-changed young daughter, made into a Skeleton Woman of the sea who is unshakeable. Shiver and quake as the young man does, he cannot leave behind this strange being he has attracted. If we can muster the same authenticity our fish-seeking hunter does, we may understand how this is so like our psycho-spiritual natures.

Our fisherman doesn't seek to "get himself together". He pulls her into the very heat of his home, his own center, and she follows him there, as if stuck to his backside. In a sense she is, because the entanglement of their confrontation has her wound up in the fisherman's plans and very being. Still, he stays with the whole experience and the story makes space for an open, full-bodied response. This displays an ability to go through it all from beginning to end and on to the next beginning.

He appears to be dealing with the legacy of the father, a less-willing male influence which has somehow gone against nature and lost its' wetness, the very Water of Life. Now the young fisherman is forced to face the effects of his kinsfolk's and his own earlier actions, by extension of blood ties and unknowing naivety. In this fashion, the fisherman is chased by the life that has lain hidden yet remains re-animated in the fluidly shifting places just beneath everyday awareness.

In many of the dreams I've worked with, my own and others', this theme of the chase shows up. The literalist view would have us think we'd do well to outrun the chasers. It's often the case that we dream of escaping the forces that hunt after us in our dreams. We may feel triumphant relief over such escapades. In the long view, it's been my experience that we actually very often want to embody this engaging and surrendered response that our storied fisherman illustrates.

I think it's fair to say that we have often been taught that fear is a sign of weakness. The fisherman shows us otherwise. In his ability to feel what he is faced with, he is moved to the place of healing and belonging, and so is Skeleton Woman. In speaking to our collective fears about the literal end of the world in his brilliant book, *Why the World Doesn't End*, Michael Meade reminds us,

> "What we usually think of as fear is actually our response to the presence of fear; an increased heartbeat, growing anxiety, and panic are all effects of fear, not fear itself. Fear can cause hesitancy, loss of confidence, and fragmentation, but those are results of fear that has not been fully faced. Fear is an old word that derives from the same roots that give us "fare", as in "thoroughfare". Although it often causes people to run away from troubling situations, at a

deeper level fear means "to go through it". The hidden purpose of fear involves bringing us closer to natural instincts for survival, but also for awakening to inner resources and sharpening our intelligence when faced with true danger and the basic need to change."[12]

Whatever else we can say or see, the fisherman honors his instincts, emotions and feelings *through* his flight. This running towards home and stopping to face what's there, allows the Skeleton Woman to feed herself for the first time in a long while, from the humanly gathered stores of drying fish. Along the path, she grabs some handfuls for her hunger. Something in this flight towards home ironically starts putting the flesh back on the bones of the Woman of the Soul. Within our hunter-fisherman, courage shines forth in the willingness to bring her into where he begins to come to terms with what and who he has encountered in the course of his hunt.

SLAKING A GREAT THIRST

Once he lights his lamp – a lucid bringing of the warmth of fire and hence, awareness – the lone fisherman begins to capably act upon the grief that has been visited upon this former little daughter. She is his own soul, on one important level. As we've noted in our discussion of Dummling, folk tales reveal the way that the one who is as yet unscathed by the all-too-tempting attitudes of calculated skepticism, is the one who has yet enough trust to bumble forth into the exact place of sought after redemption. Somewhere in every heart, there may exist the spark of this uncovered recognition of what has been and gets eaten away.

Our trusty hunter lights a further fire in the hearth and a flame in the heart is also kindled into flowering out of the soil of death and fear. This fiery heat becomes the tenderness that is able to cook the longed for tears that have yet to be shed over the suffering and the wound caused to She-Who-Must-Be-Remembered-Back-To-Life, and equally, the little human daughter become woman. Some serious alchemy is well under way now, wherein the relating between these potencies is having healing effects.

How similar to modern everyday life this all is when we look from a certain angle! The earth, the nature of trees, bees and blossoms, the krill blooms in the oceans and the ever-renewing well-springs of forests and grasses spread out across the many rich and vital domains of the ground we walk upon and amongst have, for many ages, borne a quality of this young feminine energy cast away into the sea. Every time a forest is cleared, or oil is spilled in the ocean, whenever military sonar in sea-going war vessels are favored over the needs and wild natures of whales and all the living creatures of the vital matrix of the planet, human beings cut away at and dismember the flesh of the young daughters and the womanly powers of the natural world.

Also present and true, in the story and potentially in our response to The Woman of the Soul in The Womb of the World, is the strengthening that visits and expands her very being – out of a kind of death, into the bloom of a woman from the bud of a girl. This is the magic that occurs when we allow our selves to get caught into the business of remembering. These are the womanly, feminine wiles of bringing life back to life, which men also bear within our selves, of birthing and rebirthing out of kinds of death and destruction. It's not one in favor of the other, however. We don't want to make the mistake of skipping past the struggle by only seeing and seeking the rebirth. We do all contain these seeds of growth and death that feed one another in several vital shapes in our own beings and in our world. When we really give over to the dying and the pain, then will come in their own time, the renewal and transformation. But we can't have one without the other – it's a package deal.

Something about this cyclical turning condition is also related to our human consumption and endless hunger, our tendency to trample down, thrash and tear apart the living world about us for the seeking of shelter, continuance, nurturance and further still, in the name of "progress". Still, if we're willing to bring Skeleton Woman home, into the very center of our lives, to acknowledge the pain and wounding and to become the grief that goes into sustaining ourselves and could go into sustaining the life and death about and within us, we may yet find a real song to sing.

Such a song conjures a pool of salt-seasoned tears to shed and a cleansing fire to burn that helps bring life back to life, to remember soul and the woman within and without, to creatively, imaginatively sing and drum the very flesh of her body and our own wisdom, knitting belonging back in to life, also vitally aware of the necessity and import of death.

For, the young daughter has visited Death on her quest, which leads up to this moment in the ice hut of the fisherman. He himself has begun to know death in his witnessing the Skeleton Woman as he does, and in his going through and facing the fear and grief that comes as a result. The story implies, symbolically at least, though we can also embody this energy and see it as an actuality in our lives and the world, that the two are about the business of going across thresholds that acquaint each with the Life-Death-Life design. The little daughter has clearly changed through her ordeal. The fisherman can now no longer make the same claim to his former identity of being naïve and innocent.

The eloquence of native, indigenous wisdom to be found in the story is so simple yet so profound. The young, new and growing potentials for all our lives and for life itself inevitably gets torn to its core. Yet *we must remember and witness this* and find ways to live this truth, so that we may pull our own deepest hearts into the kind of care that can arouse the singing back to life of that which we have thrown away, forgotten, eaten and neglected. We might not have known that we bear such a relation to our very own souls and the soul of all that is in Nature and the world until we acknowledge how we are living our own version of the tale. This is akin to the young hunter who is now stirred to shed his naïve stance in favor of a much more embodied act. Still, the return of the woman wouldn't be what it is if she wasn't also brought to the threshing floor of her bony exile that lasts who knows how long. This needs to occur within men as well as women in actual life too.

The fisherman *remembers* the Woman-of-Life-Death-Life, in the face of this ribald confrontation. In running homeward, he brings it all back home. He could have tried to avoid the situation and gone to sleep in the dark and hoped for some other "out" from all this challenge. He also could have run elsewhere and tried to shake the entanglement and leave the skeleton far from where he lives. Fair play to our fisherman, however, because he shows us that it's desirable to do otherwise.

He compassionately begins singing whilst in the Woman of the Souls midst. Something in him can't help but to begin seeking to arrange her bones in the way they ought to go and to offer her whatever fortune has presented him with previously, as he covers her in the furs he's got stored in his home.

Since we've invoked a word that is used often these days, let's be sure that we know what is being said. *Compassion* grows from the roots wherein "passio" holds the meaning of *suffering* in ancient Greek. To have compassion, therefore, is *to suffer with*; "com" here can be understood to mean *with*. There's more salt in this word than we normally acknowledge, just as there is in our weeping, and thereby there is also more of an opening to gritty actions, feelings and sensations. We sense the fisherman's compassion, which sprouts from his willingness to be with the suffering of the Skeleton Woman, evoked by his own capacity for grief. The word suffering means, according to its' roots, *to go under*. Isn't that what the little daughter had to do? Isn't that how she became the Skeleton Woman for a time? By opening to compassion, the fisherman goes under with the Woman of the Soul, and through this salty, wet, deathly, connective facing up. As a result, a portion of The Song of Life is shaken loose and enlivens both. This is not the detached version of compassion we may know of in popular parlance today where the one who has suffered is told to "move past the pain and let go of your attachments", or worse, "let go of your story and all will be well".

The truth of things is being brought home now. In the story, we witness exactly what is called for in our individual and collective lives today. If, on some level, we could all see our selves as the fisherman, frightened by what we've discovered, yet willing to bring the paradoxical treasure of this truth into the very centers of our lives, our homes, our hearts, our town squares and the many places where we live, work and die we could belong. If we could also see and find our selves in the Skeleton Woman who has made herself known to us and who has tracked us to the very foundations of our myriad existences, we might trust that a surrender to her and to the truths of what we've forgotten are the very sources of actual healing that we've been seeking all along.

The tale, at this point, speaks to how the tear Skeleton Woman drinks from the fisherman's cheek as he slips into his surrendered sleep is sprung from a dream. It's as if the elixir of wholeness producing waters can only come from this place of trust, wounding and visionary experience. The fisherman has now given over to a larger-than-ordinary-life-power by sinking into a special sleep across from Skeleton Woman. She herself may only be brought back to life with such tears, along with other ingredients that are essential to her being reborn in fully human, though spirited form. It's as if the man now actually does go under, and in the salt of his dreaming, suffers his own immersion beneath the waves of slumber's ocean. He so fully witnesses the state of this woman, that he has no choice but to go down to face himself.

Skeleton Woman, born from a fallen little daughter, now sings as she reaches into the fisherman's breast to handle his heart once he is in this place of collapse. The road of song towards the hut of healing is full of the rhythm and feeling to be found in this organ, which, we moderns seem to have forgotten, daily and nightly provides the percussive soundtrack without which we wouldn't even be alive.

Pinkola-Estes majestically speaks to this power of the muse in reflecting upon the healing vitality found in sound,

"Singing is considered to issue from a mysterious source, one that enwisens the whole of creation, all the animals and the humans and the trees and the plants and all who hear it... The creation hymn produces psychic change. The tradition of such is vast: there are love-producing songs in Iceland, and among the Wichita and Micmac. In Ireland, a magic power is called down by magic song. In one Icelandic story, a person falls on the ice crags and severs a limb, but is regenerated through the signing of song."[13]

The heart is a great center of human emotion and feeling. There's much wisdom in this pulsing cadence. The supportive beating of the heart is a kind of foundation for our existence that melodiously rides upon the grounded roots of such a carrying power. Drumming moves us. The point would seem to be to get moved by heart to the proper place of belonging. Dancing, unexpected artfulness and singing are included in the price of admission.

The fact that The-Woman-Who-Fell-And-Now-Rises-Again sings to the fisherman's heart, imparts to us that it is not only she who is in need of some soothing, tender yet strength-filled expression. She is also singing a whole new intelligence into the lonely hunter. This is one way grief is a doing, not just a feeling. In addition to his having fallen asleep, the cajoling of his heart by this Woman of the Soul, who is now relocating a place of human belonging, shows us that the wound of "the fathers" is visited upon each one of us. The masculine, He-Who-Fishes-Daily-For-Finding-True-And-Actual-Sustenance, also suffers a pain to the heart when She-Whose-Eyes-Drink-And-Reflect-The-Ocean, is cast down and away.

Let us also observe, at last, that the mothers don't appear in the story to stop the original act of that first father. Why is this? Perhaps the story shows us that the mothering powers are to be found in the oceanic place of forgetting and remembering. This is the place where the little daughter has gone and is returning from with a totally renewed capacity for calling life back to life (amid an ability to learn from a form of death), in concert with the equally renewing energies of the manly fisherman. The mothers may have more to do with pain and the descent than we realized, and maybe this is why they don't appear to stop any of this when it all gets under way, at the very beginning.

WHEN SPIRIT IS CALLED DOWN, BODY RISES UP

This great little storied adventure bespeaks a divine play between human experience and the inter-weaving of a deeper, wider, ever-returning nature than the one which modernity has sought to impress upon us. As the flesh re-appears on Skeleton Woman's body, the soul and the spirit have now found a place of trustworthiness. The gift the hunter naturally feels moved to give when faced with her presence is returned and deepened by her, and by the experience that has informed and fed both of them.

The fisherman can be intuited as the inner man of the womanly identities to be found in the little daughter turned Skeleton Woman, who shape-shifts into a maturing woman. She has found her own powers of worthiness in herself as well. This is played out in the action of the intoning of her body back upon her frame. There are whole other strata connected to this spiral of amplification.

By coming together in the way that they do, we see how both woman and man enjoy the gifts of the life-sustaining mothering powers of the ocean and the great mysterious. In the end the pair receive a lifelong bounty from the sea itself. This is the true blessing of the joining of the powers of human attention able to relate with the wilding and cyclic forces, and of the ocean-as-unconscious, the underworld nature. There is a conjoining here too, with the strange yet desirable dance between seeming opposites, woman and man, life and death, flesh and memory, nature and culture, known and unknown.

The fathering powers equally appear to be reborn in a helpful fashion in the tale. The willingness to fish for the truth, on the hunters' part, is an aspect of the outward going, ever-searching quality of the Man-Inside-Each-Of-Us. That action of going out and risking oneself in the world has a classically masculine quality to it; yet this energy is incomplete without the womanly nature, which we can see is strong and also fierce. In fact, the feminine has been out there in the wild much more deeply in this story, than the fisherman has. Both have the ability to encounter and relate to the untamed, and both bear responsibility for relating with forces found in the outer world. The flight homeward suggests the way that the inner is also of great value and offers us a hint about digesting the adventures we encounter within the strange cradling-destroying arms of the everyday.

The scene inside this humble, duende filled ice hut involves the singing back to a human, enfleshed state for the Skeleton Woman. This is the return from the rites of a heroine's trial of tribulations. Symbolically and therefore also actually, this is the embodiment of a soulful, spirited nature in the body – for the fisherman as well. The singing of the flesh back on the bones can be understood as the intelligence of the DNA seeds in Lady Death-Life-Death's bones, co-creating a healing ceremony. Even though the story images this human woman's return, we also sense a wider cycle. And a return of the leaves and branches, the blossoming sprouts of the forest, the harmonious and sensitive balance of the ocean temperatures and the sky's fragile and divinely balanced energies being found whole again in a wild Spring bloom of the return of the Holy in Nature. All these essentials are fed by Death, tended through a panoply of actions and feelings, by deep movements of the psyche and the physical world. Spirit and matter are powerfully interwoven in the story and its events.

The replenishing of the flesh on the bones in the tale is akin to a deeply felt, sensed and acknowledged reforming of the body of human culture itself, imbued by the soul of this advent, and also the sensuous action that can flow naturally from authentic love for our selves, the wild and one another. When a woman and a man (or a man and a man, a woman and a woman) can join together in this way, new life can be seeded amid a rhythm of great joy, grief, recognition and pleasure that echoes out in waves of beauty, pulled by tidal swells in the actions of Skeleton Woman and the fisherman as they sing each others hearts out and bodies back to life in the story, and in our imaginations.

In dreams, too, when lovers come together, when there is merely a suggestion at sexual-sensual activity, the message of experience always has to do with how we might understand the comingling of seemingly disparate energies. The actual experience of the metaphor and reality of sex ultimately serves as a reinforcement of the joining together with the energies of the Divine in Nature: Spirit, Soul and the surrender that is possible in the embodiment of our most stripped away sensibilities for ecstatic union. To join with our opposite, is to embrace the inner and outer opposition of life and death.

In a multitude of sacred traditions, from alchemy to Tibetan Buddhism and on to Jungian teachings, one of the devotional aims of the work is to undergo just such a pairing. Encounters in the waking world evoke this coming together. So do our engagements in psychic landscapes, stories, dreams and the imagination. Such couplings constitute a marriage of seemingly opposed characters and qualities.

In alchemical practice it's called the "coniunctio" or the sacred marriage that is so often hinted at in dreams. This is one of the reasons that so many fairy stories end with weddings – to show that we are continually invited to come together with all of who and how we are and can be, with *all that is seemingly not us*, each man also a woman and each woman also a man.

Through this marriage, the trustworthy fisherman and the tender, grief-soaked fierce woman also involve other elements that have brought shape to the action in the tale. This is a wedding of fears, a redemption of the throwing away, the call to ordinary adventure, the ordeal and the return, as much as it is a conjoining of the elements within which the story takes place – the ocean, the ice, the sun, the hunt, the entanglement, the fire, the hearth, the creatures that live within and co-create the sea, the sky, the clouds, the village and the life of the two-leggeds on land.

In our tale, we've witnessed the regaining of vital relationships that were somehow lost and are now brought back into the ken of deep care. The story doesn't suggest that it's an easy, only blissful or peaceful ride. It shows that such a quest engages all the aspects of our own being, our own belonging, in a wild world that reflects the many living forces of a natural domain in which we too may make every effort to come back into union. We engage this pursuit by exploring the mysterious depths inside and out, fishing for the wisdom, beauty and revitalization that are possible when we tend a daily-nightly effort at communicating with the forgotten and watery sides of who and how we are and how others are.

This story is crucial for describing a sense of recognizing the necessity for acknowledging and giving to the "other". The Other is anyone, plant, animal, man, woman, rock, wave, city building that we may witness and experience as "not us" or "not me". At the same time that we can confirm our connection to "inner forces" by seeing that we are all women and men on some level, we are also bidden not to make everything and everyone into a narcissistic extension of our selves. There's a paradox to this. Such a quality points to a move through and past either/or thinking and feeling into both/and understandings. In other words, the very real sense that the fisherman is caring for and getting to know the "woman within and without" is part of the teaching the tale details. At the same time, and in addition to this perceivable psychic fact, it's also true that the Little-Daughter-Turned-Skeleton-Woman who yet again becomes a human lover and wife is also who she is: she is a separate being who has her own nature, her own gifts, frailties and wondrously unique, distinct capacities. The Other is separate, yet not, uniquely its own being, and yet on some level, the selves and the others of the world are also deeply interwoven and interconnected as "one". *The One is in the Many and the Many are in the One*, so to speak.

Relating and belonging are indebtedness to the natural world that surrounds and cradles us. Through a felt-sense of dearly placed respect for the energies that inevitably bring us to the thresholds of death and life and reveal in an on-going cycle of many forces leading us to the Other, the story shows how we might also feed and be fed by the psycho-spiritual living energies of our deepest natures and Nature itself. This nourishment occurs amid the embracing of our own wild spirits and souls, as well as the vital and often fearsome spirits to be found in this original place we've been entrusted to belong within. Might we not therefore seek to make and be made into real human beings through the course of our lives and brushes with death?

Ultimately, the story unveils a more complete yet expansive set of vital truths, just like dreams do when we honor their beckonings toward learning. We are not alone. The mighty forces within, which we can locate ourselves, with help, have a hugely important hand in how we craft and are crafted by existence as human beings. We could find that everyone is alive and soaked in grief as well as joy, amid the expansive, mysterious, yet often knowable domains of our experience, held in a truly witnessed place of belonging by much that is felt and understood as larger-than-life, yet which also includes real limits and a true sense of smallness, all-at-once.

Endnotes Chapter 6

---

[1] Jeremy Taylor, The Living Labyrinth, 1998, Paulist Press, New Jersey, p. 11

[2] Martin Shaw, A Branch from the Lightning Tree, 2011, White Cloud Press, Ashland Oregon, p. 7

[3] Martin Shaw, A Branch from the Lightning Tree, 2011, White Cloud Press, Ashland Oregon, p. 27

[4] Marion Woodman and Robert Bly, The Maiden King: The Reunion of Masculine and Feminine, 1998, Henry Holt, p.177

[5] Clarissa Pinkola Estes, Women Who Run with the Wolves, 1992, Ballantine, New York, p.141

[6] Michael Meade, Fate and Destiny, the Two Agreements of the Soul, 2010, Green Fire Press, p.79-80

[7] Marie-Louise Von Franz, The Interpretation of Fairy Tales, Revised Edition, 1996, Shambala, Boston, p.64

[8] Andreas Lommel, Shamanism: The Beginings of Art, 1967 New York, McGraw Hill Books, p.56

[9] Mircea Eliade, Rites and Symbols of Initiation, 1958, Harper Collins, p. 92

[10] Jeremy Taylor, The Living Labyrinth, 1998, Paulist Press, New Jersey, p. 133

[11] Marie-Louise von Franz, Projection and Re-collection in Jungian Psychology, Reflections of the Soul, 1995, Open Court Publishing, p.162-163

[12] Michael Meade, Why the World Doesn't End, 2012, Green Fire Press, Seattle WA, p.43-44

[13] Clarissa Pinkola Estes, Women Who Run with the Wolves, 1992, Ballantine, New York, p.160

Introduction to Part II,
Dream Songs on the Road of Life and Death

"When the words we want to use shoot up of themselves – we get a new song"
Orpingalik, Netsilik Eskimo

Some of the most pressing challenges of our times revolve around the issue of how the earth that we live upon and the world within which we exist are rapidly changing and may be seen as threatened. The many creatures of this world, the plant people, the animals, the waters, the shifting soils beneath us, and the very air and sky we breathe are considered by many to be at risk. Ecologists, environmental activists and a bevy of scientists report that large numbers of species are currently going extinct everyday. Extinct, according to what we can see and tend to assume as human beings, means *forever*.

While nature can be clearly felt as besieged, many culture wars rage across the planet throughout the modern landscape. The more extreme outer conditions appear to be, the more folks seem to dig in and look for some notion of fundamental certainty about the right position to take, even where the position might look like no position at all. In North America the now familiar battles are waged between the 'right' and the 'left', conservatives who don't seem too concerned about conservation and liberals who may become ever more focused on structures that seem to promise unlimited freedom. Has anyone asked the earth and her creatures how they feel about what's happening?

Where I live with my small family, on our farm in Northern California, we've recently had a winter storm visit us that has flooded many nearby areas to the point where people have been filmed on the news traveling down main streets in kayaks. Despite this apocalyptic flood of rain, we've been experiencing one of the most intense droughts in recorded history. It would appear that ours truly is a time of extremes. We go from the deluges of isolated big storms to the ravages of the wildfire seasons, from one end of a spectrum to the other, and rapidly. The climate of the weather would seem to mimic the political poles and the mostly unacknowledged inner terrain of human psyches.

I could list a number of examples, and yet I think we all likely have a sense of how truly intense modern life has become – whether we are acting on that grief and acknowledging it is another question. In various ways, for many the timeworn mantras of "life goes on" and "I gotta take care of my own" rule the day.

"What are we to do?" are words that form within many hearts and upon many lips throughout the contemporary scenes of modern life. According to Michael Meade in his *Why the World Doesn't End,* there are likely to be two guiding mythologies that form the backdrop of our age. These mythos pertain to our sense of belonging and are related to the perceived endings of time, what he terms the archetype of "apocalypse". On one hand we can see the now familiar contemporary idea of ever-increasing progress – *ascent*, endless development and action. On the other is the perception and experience of *decline*, the mythic equivalent of "The End", utter and complete collapse.

As we've seen during our exploration in Part I, the old stories and the energies of our dreams put us back in touch with deep, soulful, imaginative and creative possibilities for bringing life back to life and for honoring, experiencing and seeking to know the energies of death. The imaginal realities of dream, story, art and our work with these make space for a less one-sided approach to the ancient experience of the paradoxical cosmic and human forces of *Creation-Destruction-Creation*. The wise images, symbols and scenarios of our dreams and storytelling traditions, along with many of our creative disciplines remind us that some on-going drama threaded deep into the fabric of "Life on Earth" may faithfully clothe those of us who seek to craft a life here amidst the confusing, beautiful, heartbreaking and ever-challenging cornucopia of situations encountered in this waking world.

We appear to live in a time where the extreme interests of existence veer on the edges of those very same archetypal, and hence, timeless powers of advancement and breakdown. Some folks have pledged to return to nature, to put time, energy and focus into redeeming the wild world about and within. Other folks seem to feel and think that the gifts of technology offer the most familiarity and promise and believe that the way to deal with the ills of life is to be resolved through further development of the very machines and gizmos that seem to be, at least in part, behind the whole dilemma.

One view of what's around the next corner tends to reveal a vista of immense collapse. This alternative idea presents a form of some kind of science fiction futurity. As mind and heart tend towards the natural psychic attractions of polarity, one possible future looks like a time wherein all the machines fail and are reclaimed by the natural forces that they somehow sprang from not so very long ago. Another vision may be found in a kind of ever-developing drama wherein artificial environments created by human beings form a techno-future that ever recedes from the natural world as we've known and inhabited it. This second view is of a kind of electronic world where humans and our inventions battle it out for meaning, survival and validity, forsaking Great Nature in the pursuit of comfort, security and long lives.

This latter scene has the continuation of species extinction and global climate change eventuating a reality wherein the very technologies we've created continue to more fully subsume the overall reality and tone of planetary and natural life. Still other eyes and imaginations may simply see a static continuation of the status that life could appear to be existing within at the very moment – "life as usual". Yet if we are honest, history has shown us that change is the only thing that ever stays the same, as a well-worn cliché would have it. In other words, change will come, like it or not. Are we headed towards "more of the same", a surprising return to the magnificence of a wilding and natural existence, or a sci-fi version of a machine-driven and digital world akin to visions to be found in such films as *Blade Runner* or *The Matrix*? Maybe there are other, more complicated and unexpected possibilities that we can help to co-create, that don't exactly conform to such either/or, black or white scenarios. After all, where might the so-called Middle Path lie amid the far-stretching poles of extremity we can so clearly see and feel in our lives today?

Perhaps the mystery of existence poses us with such edge-fostering questions to give us fuel for the authentic living of our lives. It does appear to be true that it's possible to draw upon and receive the potent and intelligent experience and messages in our dreams. We may do this as a means for seeking the beginnings of answers that can show us how the ancient energies of Creation-Destruction-Creation can in/form our very human efforts at reimagining lives worth living and deaths worth dying. Our dreams, stories and abilities to create – whether we are evoking the artful forms to be found in painting, innovating, music- making, architecture, gardening, healing and many other practices that involve our total beings and the natural order that we're so deeply threaded by and into – put us in relation to the idea of myth as "the dream of place".

The more we open up to our dreams and visions, the more we will notice, that "everything is alive". By working with our imaginations, we become able to envision a future (and a 'present') worth inhabiting – for the ones who are coming behind us and who came before us, the Elders and the Youth of the plant nations, the people nations, the rock nations, the water nations and the animal nations.

It's been my experience that working with dreams and certain kinds of sound in groups is a potent craft for approaching the kinds of relationships, with each other and the vital world around us, that have the practical ability to help us to hold, exist within and learn from what Jungians call *the tension of opposites*.

Rilke says,

"Just as the winged energy of delight carried you over
many chasms early on,
now raise the daringly imagined arch
holding up the astounding bridges.

Miracle doesn't lie only in the amazing
living through and defeat of danger;
Miracles become miracles in the clear
achievement that is earned.

To work with things is not hubris,
when building the association beyond words;
denser and denser the pattern becomes –
being carried along is not enough.

Take your well-disciplined strengths
and stretch them between two poles.
Because inside human beings
is where Goddesses and Gods learn.

Many of us may be hoping for some existing social structure to come up with solutions to our problems. Isn't this what governments, churches and universities are supposed to provide? Somehow these cultural bodies have all given way to big business and the seemingly inviolable institutionally defined bodies we call corporations. Are any of these socially created constructs effectively serving the actual needs of people, animals, plants, elements and the planet?

In his visionary book, *The Mist-Filled Path*, a work focused on regaining the roots of Celtic Spirituality, Frank MacEowen speaks to this situation. The following passage reflects his assessment,

> "Traditions, religions, economies, and systems of governing that do not acknowledge the sentience of our planet cannot be sustained. For us, as individuals and communities who comprise the microcosm of these greater systems, it is an act of mental health, a humanitarian investment in healing the future, to openly question the wisdom and sustainability of... antiquated institutions. We must shake ourselves from the myopic view that our individual choices do not have an impact."[1]

Perhaps, as dream explorations and wisdom seeking practices strongly suggest, each one's role is to become fully oneself and then to belong as that, giving one's gifts fully in each surrounding community. When we sincerely pay attention to voices in the body, voices in our dreams, voices of wisdom reaching out to us from the wild and natural world, our Ancestors and the living creatures that surround us with vibrant storied existences, we inevitably recognize that *we are nature too*. The practice is not without its challenges to be sure.

Throughout time we have been and will be constantly re-invited to imagine our way through the various tragedies, joys, traumas, successes and dilemmas of our ever-unfurling lives.

Maybe the best that we can each do is to become ourselves, who we are meant to be according to the surprising yet deeply knowable design of the sacred in the soul and in nature. As we apprentice ourselves to this task, we may become students of the imagination – our vital ability to dream and be dreamt up as beings belonging to our riskiest creations and destructions – wherein we are called to carry out the heart-rending twists and turns appearing at the crossroads of our own and each others' lives.

UNLIKELY OFFERINGS
BEAR THE WEIGHT OF THE WORLD

We seem to be so far away from knowing what it is, exactly, that we can do to make an offering of thanks that might lead to living the kind of life that could redeem the thriving life-forms and beings that have given so much of themselves in order to feed and support us. What can we give Nature that She-He doesn't already have? The answer might lie in our own uniqueness, our very humanness. The old cultures of many peoples around the world have known this throughout time. This is why traditional ways of living have included for ceremonial practices that draw upon the beauty of human feeling, action, eloquence, hand-made sacrifices and offerings as well as music and poetry that are capable of feeding the divine spirits of the earth, the otherworlds and the cosmos. These 'people' exist right in front of us in the bending boughs of trees and on our dinner plates in the form of plants and beasts that we take for our very sustenance.

We can see this in the prayers of many traditional cultures, the hand-woven garments and food jars that have been created many times over, in the music and dances, the expert and lovingly hewn tools and fetishes of the ancients, from Celtic to Mongolian cultures, from Mayan to ancient Nordic peoples. The true gift we have to offer as an on-going, everyday Thanksgiving can come from our efforts to utter words of grief and praise amid the deliciousness of cooking thanks in our bellies, throats, and upon the dancing wands of our flickering tongues as well with our hands and fingers that may touch, play and craft instruments for the rendering of our unique sacraments of offering. Perhaps too, some well-wrought designs for farming and architecture will come through from the connections we make to artful inner designs that are also inherent within the soul, in an effort to give back for all we take.

Cultures of many ages have made rituals involving music, well-wrought constructs and sacred sounds as a means for inviting, praising, entering and being entered by the wisdom and magnificence of great dreaming visions that have always informed a true sense of belonging. Such artful praxis has allowed the many diverse people of nature, insects, animals, trees, sea creatures and more, to make their own longings and characters known to us two-legged wanderers, exiles that we are, upon the ever-greening soils of the earth. It is through these efforts at beauty and wholeness, our Holy, Hole-filled creations that we have always found our way into a place of belonging as real human beings. Through our joyful yet lugubrious offerings, we might break out of and return from the baleful prisons of a strangely self-imposed banishment. We might still co-create connected lifeways for ourselves, and the many others we live here with via the realizations of the forgetful ways of our very own natures. What is "holy" is really a testament to the holes we leave in things as a result of what we take in order to survive during our time here.

> Emerson speaks to an awareness of belonging,
> "We lie in the lap of an immense intelligence, which makes us receivers of its truth and organs of its activity."

In a contemporary effort to revivify ancient potentials to be found in the seedbeds of our souls, we now turn to an exploration of how sound and music may become the foodstuff of our dreaming selves. This is a feeding of and for the spirits and souls of the Dreaming and of this bewildering magical and everyday world and its myriad life-forms that we cohabitate with and depend upon at so many levels. Just like the Old Ones, yet in our own way, we might unveil and give gifts that can bring forth a vibrant and expressive effort towards payback. Such an approach becomes the discipline of our seeking to fill the empty holes that our taking from the Holy manifests daily and nightly. When we honestly reflect, we may realize we'll never "make even". Even so, each of us has our own offering of being and belonging to bring and the realizing of how beholden we are can only elicit our best efforts.

These skills and true talents are witnessed through attention to the many truthful depictions that play out in our dreams and visions and are hinted at over and over in folk myths and great stories.

We may remember, like the fisherman in the tale of Skeleton Woman, how to care for and bring back to life the *spirit of the depths*. This adventure helps us to reclaim artful activities for creating health and wholeness while also providing us with devotional practices that bear the possibility for giving nourishment back to the wild worlds of dreaming and waking. This venture finds its ground in the understanding that the gifts we contain are not for us alone – they are also for the places and people we find ourselves carving out an existence within and alongside.

DREAMSOUNDING, BRIDGES BETWEEN WORLDS

As we will explore in this second part of this book, which you behold with your very own gift-laden eyes, music and sound are effective carriers for reimagining ways to honor, engage and invite our dreams, and for making offerings to the Holy in Nature. These timeless and timely elements create sacred spaces for the bringing of life back to life, and for opening to the visceral truths and hardships of dying and death.

A trusty guide I have found helpful in terms of contemplating ways to do this is Ted Andrews' *Sacred Sounds*.

Andrews offers us this guiding thought,
"… all of the ancient mystery schools taught their students the use of sound as a creative and healing force. It is considered the oldest form of healing, and it was a predominant part of the early teachings of the Greeks, Chinese, East Indians, Tibetans, Egyptians, American Indians, Mayas and the Aztecs."[2]

Some years ago, myself and a companion went on a kind of vision quest to the Big Sur wilderness of coastal Northern California. We spent several days camping and being opened to the vast beauty of this breathtaking on-the-edge wilderness. On one particularly blustery sunlit day, we went for a walk through the nearby meadow and into the woods, which led to large rocky vistas overlooking the mighty Pacific Ocean.

The spot we were encamped within was an open grassland not far from the rolling breakers of the vast western ocean. Heading towards the sun, listening to the long, drawn out, watery and stone-filled crash of the long-traveled waves roiling in the distance, we came to a gale-filled standing tribe of old immigrant eucalyptus trees marking the bounds between the camping glade and nearby beach. Some of these weathered denizens had trunks that could measure easily within ten to twelve feet in circumference. These leaf-filled creatures are true giants. Some spirit seemed to pull at my coat sleeves and we stopped to listen to the creek and groan of these magnificent tree people as they greeted the long-journeying gusts blowing off the surging waters & made a song of them. We simply stood awhile amidst the wagging, wending and waving of their tonguing leaves as they spoke to us from above, as well as from trunks below, issuing forth creaking moans and low-bellied, aching arboreal languages.

I had brought my didjeridu along and began to play, to make an offering to that breeze-filled wood. The droning whorl of the instrument joined the bass-filled chorus of the root-bound trees amid the unceasing march and collapse of the salty waves upon the strand just around the next bend on the trail. The Irish speak of "thin places" where portals open in this world to the worlds behind the world. We found ourselves, at that time, in such a place.

While entering a light trance, eyes closed halfway and feeling quite tranquil, I observed a nuthatch who had alighted upon my vibrating didjeridu. I've now been playing this instrument for over twenty years. To this day, that was the only time a winged creature has landed upon my instrument while I was playing. The tiny bird sat there and peered up at me and I felt the depth of a connection to that place and the spirits of nature in a way that has sustained and informed me ever since.

Our "fine feathered friend" trusted us to get close enough to breathe the same air and to get a good true look at one another. I continued to play for something like ten minutes and this bird remained there until I finished. I had the distinct intuition that this was the forests way of expressing interest and gratitude for the music, for the song. A way the spirits have for saying, "We hear you... we appreciate and honor what we hear and feel."

I never quite picked apart or poked at that memorable moment. Yet I know this was an omen of acknowledgement of the wild, a deep soul connection which was expressing itself through the dream of that place, comingling with an offering to it in the form of contemplation, respect, feeling and sound. This encounter showed me how I have gifts to give Nature. I give thanks to that bird and to that wood to this day. For, along with the ocean and the wind, the sun and the soil, they helped teach me that it is possible to live within the mythos of our own lives, and within the matrix of the mythology of Nature that we are certainly beholden to and are invited to come into relation with throughout the course of our lives here on this grace-filled earth.

Similar moments are available to each of us, if we will open ourselves to the dreaming awareness that is able to teach us how truly interconnected we are with one another. We may inhabit such moments of relatedness that move across the lines of distinctions that we have created, which falsely suggest we are separate, which yet describe such wonderful differences at the same time.

Let us turn now, with this story in mind and close at heart, to an exploration of how we might open more fully to the dream of our lives and deaths and of the forces that sustain, support and inform us and Great Nature herself in ways that we may have only begun to imagine. Let us carry the notion that we are capable of apprenticing ourselves to a "dream of place", in our efforts to connect with the living, dying, surprising, breathtaking beauty that surrounds us and which we may seek to give back to, offering gratitude and pragmatic acts for the many gifts of this fulsome, human, ensouled and spirited, interwoven existence.

Endnotes, Introduction to Part II

---

[1] Frank MacEowen, "The Mist-Filled Path, Celtic Wisdom for Exiles, Wanderers and Seekers", 2002, New World Library, Novato, California, p.118

[2] Ted Andrews, "Sacred Sounds, Magic & Healing Through Words and Music", 2008,
Llewellyn Publications, Woodbury, MN, p.3

CHAPTER 7

Sound, Dreaming, Soul and Spirit

"All art is capable of duende. But the place that it naturally occurs is in music, dance or spoken poetry..."
Federico Garcia Lorca

Working with sound and dreams together manifests a uniquely balanced and beauty-laden path towards wholeness and soul. Drawing upon ideas and discussion about dreams may be brought to bear while seeking to relate with deep mysteries of being, becoming and belonging. Yet what of the body and alternate ways of honoring the dreams as well as the meanings, which they seek to impart, that may invite a complimentary approach? What of the sensations and feelings that dreaming and reflecting on dreams arouses?

In bringing music to dream explorations, subtle yet physically real elements may also be involved, with the use of various instruments and the human voice. Emotional territories come to the fore amid musical efforts at making a reception for dreams and their energies. While holding a visionary awareness, dreams and other experiences called forth out of memory can be ripened and opened to in a more fulsome manner when sound is invoked. This practice of *dream sounding* serves as a tool for allowing a less exclusively thinking-based approach towards the dreams as well as our entire lives, awake and asleep.

As playful, artistic disciplines, sound and music afford the dreams ensouled pathways for approaching us. Recalling dreams, sharing them as personal and collective guiding folk-myths and contemplating them in a flow of sound, unexpected portals are lifted open. In this way, intuitions may be opened to and made use of in a capacious exploration of the imagination, imbued by the assistance of the Muses.

Dreams and sound, awash in certain forms of musical vibration, emotion, feeling, memory and experience, reverberate with a spirited yet soulful and even sensual essence. Sound forms waves that are absorbed, emanated, interpreted and received by our eardrums, minds, bodies, souls and hearts. Visions reach us while we sleep or surrender waking awareness. Although our imaginal experiences feature 'seen' realities of a sort, they also bear the quality of a near invisibility or mystique that tends to defy overt evident physical sensation and reality, as we know these in waking life. By honoring the similarities that exist between them, music, sound and the psyche can be brought together via the connective tissues of the imagination, our organ for witnessing that which may evade our material sense of measurement and definition.

To imagine is to cast into images. Images exist in varying forms, related to what is seen or visualized. However, some images exist as sounds, *aural imagos*, and yet others may be felt or perceived and not seen or heard. Dreaming and imagining can be understood as one in the same - a purposeful, limited yet boundless activity, an experience of engaging with imaginal realities, witnessing spirit realms, soulful experiences, storied artful worlds and beings that slip past or through waking categories.

There is and has been a long-held relationship between music of a certain sort and dreaming. R.J. Stewart reminds us,

> "From the primal and early cultures in which music was a collective and holistic response to intimations of a shared consciousness, a unified and dreamlike music arose."[1]

One can witness such realities in action by listening to the wonderful and dream-soaked recordings of music made by the Temiar people of Malaysia, cousins to the well-renowned and dream-wise Senoi folk. The Temiar behold healing energies that are given in the form of songs in their dreams. These attentive, in touch people recall their dreams, then play and perform songs received in the dreamworld in and for their communities and for the individuals within them. Thus, the energy of the dream is brought forth into this waking world while the dream spirits are honored, given voices and evoked. Their practices of healing revolve around and spring from the songs they receive via spirits in dreams. A well-recorded and highly enjoyable album called *Temiar Dream Healing* is available from Smithsonian Folkways. Anthropologist Marina Roseman has also written a thorough book exploring and documenting the culture, methods and practices of the Temiar, called *Healing Sounds From the Malaysian Rainforest*. We might learn something about how to creatively engage and honor our own healing by studying and seeking to learn from these astute dreamers from Malaysia.

DREAMS ARE MORE THAN VISUAL IMAGERY

Dreams and music not only bring us visions, but also deep feelings, sensations, emotions and knowledge. Emotion and feeling in dreams provide a crucial key for unlocking doorways to how we may seek to understand, honor and enter the dreams, unveiling important messages for our lives and the life that surrounds and feeds us and which we may, in turn, seek to feed with our creations. Music too, composed of sound as elements that form the soul, bones, flesh and skin of song, evokes and inspires an emotional, spirited and feeling-toned set of realities. The feeling realm is one that we know, but is also an experience that can be described as *non-physical* or as *subtly physical*. Biologically, it may be possible to locate the chemical changes inside our bodies that accompany the emotional shifts and feeling landscapes that we witness and co-create. Still, for the most part, we simply understand that when we feel and experience a sadness or a joy, a grief or fear, these states exist, whether we see them and can touch their beings or not. This is much like both dreams and sound, is it not?

We may accept the veracity of our emotions and our dreams, in large part, due to the felt-experience and hunch that they are real, because we have an immediate contact with them, albeit of a mysterious and hard to 'prove' sort. Music is similar, in that we hear it, and know that it's bona fide, even when we don't see the vibrations that are issuing forth.

Bringing specific forms of sound to a labor of love for understanding, receiving and feeling into our dreams creates a lively portal to other layers of our ability to experience the tones and richness of *inner* and *outer* occurrences.

This may be a misleading way of describing, or a deeply imaginative one. For, what do we mean when we speak of "inner" and "outer"? Is this the creation of a false designation that separates and divides us from our experiences and each other unnecessarily?

I like to think of *inner* and *outer* as helpful or useful fictions. "Outer" tends to refer to that which is expressed, visible and known by many. "Inner" is a direction of mystery and inwardly drawn energies that we could say are subtly perceivable and may be witnessed as highly personal, though they can be seen and felt as equally universal. These ways of describing may be related to the question of "where do dreams take place"? In the end, maybe the alchemists and astrologers who say, "As it is within, so it is without" are correct. If this is the case, and can be felt, sensed or perceived, then the separation can be healed and we might create an undivided sense of self and other in our true imaginings and waking experiences. Music and dreams are both profound aids in this practice as both are real yet elude simple or obvious categorizations. They also both invite us to acknowledge the reality of much more elusive yet also verifiable qualities and truths.

As Monika Wikman has eloquently written in the pages of her work on alchemy and psyche *Pregnant Darkness*,

"Each of us on a dream-path can learn to discover how to awaken to the inner music inside all creation and to change fluidly in response to the depths that speak to us."[2]

Discussing dreams, letting their advents ripen and dance upon our tongues, in our minds and through our hearts as we share them with one another, turning them over and gazing at them from different directions, and being held by or holding their images helps bring them to life in new and different ways for ourselves, one another and the living-dying world about us. Even though we can see how our dreams may be partially composed of ideas and experiences that we've previously culled within this lifetime, there are also clear examples of how animals, trees, stones and city buildings we've never met before also visit us as actual living and autonomous beings in our dreams. Talking about their possible meanings, messages and origins, more fully welcoming their actual energies and personalities, identities and images, we circle around helpful explorations about how we might open more deeply and fully to their gifts of experience, as well as the symbolic resonance they hold for us, and all of living creation. At the same time, unless we are full of care, we can also mistakenly place theories or conscious ideas on the dreams and forget to listen to their own voice in the effort to realize knowledge, being and perception while paying homage to their underworld dynamics of living, dying, rebirthing, belonging and vital guiding forces.

Just as with certain experiences of music, if and when we analyze those moments, if we do so in such a way as to "pin them down" we may unwittingly trample them beneath our feet. The Talmud says, "The best interpretation of a dream is the dream itself". Isn't that true of a great song as well? Who would want or need to dissect a heart-rending blues ballad or a Leonard Cohen lyric? At the same time, we might discuss and appreciate these wonders by "riffing off of" their meaning-soaked affections and messages in our mindful hearts and miraculous bodies.

DREAMSOUNDING INSTRUMENTS

Sound of a meditative and trance-inducing sort crafts passageways. It does so on several levels, in essential living fashions, spinning pathways to the symbolic spontaneous energies of dreams while we're awake, and as a consequence may influence our sleeping dreams. Music of this sort also emboldens us to connect awarenesses between the shores of wakefulness and across the many mysterious waters to the far banks of the dreaming where we spend about a third of our lives while we slumber.

Contemplative and intentionally wrought music also helps us to plant dream seeds while we're awake, for imbibing more deeply in the imaginal during nighttime dreaming experiences. When we intend to receive certain dreams or dream guidance, the effort can be greatly enhanced with the aid of musical conjurations. It's a bit like the old troubadours who courted those they loved with music through an open window at night, calling out in the spirit of longing, soul and adoration under the silvery gaze of the moon and the dying light of distant stars.

The Native American flute has been played in such a manner, cajoling people, winds, messengers and creatures, for gently and lovingly cracking open the dying seeds of dreams waiting to come back to life. This gorgeous instrument has been and still is played towards the courtship of nature and for wooing the heart of a partner. Such offerings show us how, through music, one can be serious, beauty-bound and committed, yet also willing to draw upon the arts of heart-felt expression in order to communicate and find playful though serious intimacy. Crafting sound in this way is a seeking to bring life back to life, to lay down the dead to the ground of dying, by offering gifts of wonder and well-honed crafts through prayers of yearning and soulful intelligences.

Playing certain instruments and singing are ways that I seek to learn about and honor the rhythms of life-death-life as they make themselves known in my forested backyard garden and upon our small rabbit farm. Farmers have done similar rituals for ages upon ages. There's a long lineage of planting and harvest songs that have been made in asking permission to take life from the fields.

One of the many instruments I use, alone and in groups, for growing dreams and receiving them, both while awake and during sleep, is the Aboriginal Australian didjeridu. The effects of the sounds that are created with the voice and the breath, as this ancient woodwind instrument becomes intimated with human utterances, are quite otherworldly yet also very grounding.

The spirit-voice of the tree that became wrought into a didjeridu, and the termites that hollowed it out join in a chorus with the ministrations of the player who must honor the instrument and these formative forces to even be able to make a worthy music with it. The root note, also called "the fundamental", comes through and forms a basis of sound, in the form of a drone. At the same time certain frequencies may be intoned over and upon, underneath and within the root, through the use of the voice, diaphragm, tongue, throat and lips. These orchestrations form a layer of what are called overtones and harmonics, which flow and swirl up above, down below and all around the fundamental note or tone. It's like an actual tree, with his or her roots sinking into the earth, reaching up skyward with eyes and tongues of leaves on branches dancing and speaking with the swirling airs, fires and waters of the elements, calling out to the sun, moon, wind, animals and rain.

The concerted vibrations that emanate from the didjeridu, form a bedrock of humming waves while higher frequencies and tonalities ride within, out of and upon that central note. Octaves of sonorous sound begin to take shape amid an expansive whirling of related but distinct musical swirls, possibly punctuated by percussive pulsations. There is certainly a multi-layered, multi-vocal, multi-dimensional quality to the experience of this instrument, both while playing it and swimming in its river of sound. This multi-dimensionality inspires and entrains a sympathetic *resonance* with the basic energetic qualities of numerous realities taking place all at once and on many levels. The character of this multi-faceted sound mimics the multi-faceted quality of dreams, as well. In dreams, layers and portions that first seemed set apart, once contemplated and turned over, unveil unexpected fibers of inter-connection and relationship.

Didjeridu (or Yidaki as it is traditionally called by the Yolngu People of Australia) is described by Aboriginal originators of the instrument as a necessary expression of the divinities of Creation and the living ground beneath our feet. Mandawuy Yunupingu, an Aboriginal didjerdu player and musician who played in the acclaimed world groove outfit Yothu Yindi and who was "Australian of the Year" in 1993 says,

> "Yidaki playing is a discipline encompassing art, music and history… Cherish the sound for it is the sound of Mother Earth."[3]

Didjeridu betokens an earthen character and spirit, made as it is, traditionally, from the trunk of a eucalyptus tree. When I play it for children, they often respond as if they can feel and sense that there is something of the primal mother coming through the sound. At the same time, through the use of the breath and the reality of its unique sound, the instruments character lends it an airy, spirited quality. The sound itself also has an animistic personality and evokes the reality and memory of fire and water, as inflected by the human voice, but also as a deep memory of the elemental forces that shaped the instrument through its actual lifetime as a tree. The spirits of rain and sun, night and day, moon and star , bird and beast- even the insect intelligence of termites, who once lived in and ate through the trunk - have all gone into crafting the variety of song and dream that didjeridu is capable of bringing forth in musical and ceremonial expression. We could call this *the dreaming of the didjeridu*!

Giving voice and listening to the vivid *non-ordinary* life in our dreams is one path towards an embodiment of totality, and one that can be helpfully shaped and midwived through resonance with the interwoven inherent personalities of living beings that didjeridu (and any other vital musical instrument) represents and plays to. In a very real sense, we too contain and inter-relate with the elemental forces of animal, mineral, water, fire, earth and air. Instincts, as we witness and express them, resemble the animal nature that still resides within each of us as humans, despite our observable so-called evolutionary differences. Perhaps the animism of the didjeridu is one way Great Nature has of seeking to stay connected and of speaking to us through the vibrating dreams of sound and the sound of dreams.

MULTIPLE LAYERS, DREAMING SOUNDS

In terms of the character and quality of the music the didjeridu makes, it is quite possible to compare its energy and effect with that of several traditions of *throat-singing*. In fact, much of what occurs with the voice while playing didjeridu is a close or exact fit with what I've heard Tuvans, Inuits and Mongolians do when they sing, as well as the, perhaps better-known, Tibetan Buddhist Monks. There's a wonderful book about healing using sound written by a medical doctor named Mitchell

Gaynor, in which the Gyutu Tibetan Choir is spoken of by religious scholar Huston Smith. I feel this passage accurately describes the potential of working with dreams and sound, together or independently:

> "They (the Tantric Monks) discovered ways ... of shaping their vocal cavities to resonate overtones to the point where those became audible as distinct tones in their own... *The religious significance of this phenomenon derives from the fact that overtones awaken numerous fields, sensed without being explicitly heard.* They stand in exactly the same relationship to our hearing as the sacred stands to our ordinary mundane lives. Since the object of worship is to shift the sacred from peripheral to focal awareness, the vocal capacity to elevate overtones from subliminal to focal awareness carries symbolic power. For *the object of the spiritual quest is precisely this: to experience life as replete with overtones that tell of a reality that can be sensed but not seen, sensed but not said, heard but not explicit.* (italics and parentheses mine)"[4]

This description fits quite wonderfully with the practice of working with dreams as well, where "the overtones awaken numerous fields" standing "in exactly the same relationship to our hearing as the sacred stands to our ordinary mundane lives." This statement by Smith sounds a lot like the projective-style dream work principles penned by Jeremy Taylor in his *Basic Dream Work Tool Kit*, which hold that "all dreams speak on multiple layers of meaning" and "no dream comes to tell you what you already know".

Although the relationship here is not a literal fit, metaphorically and symbolically, the "numerous fields" and "multiple layers" do hold a distinctly comparable and related, important quality. In working with dreams and sound, we might extend the notion and reality of the overtones to include the undertones.

The aim of the work with dreams too, is that of bringing to clarity and focus that which lies on the edges, in the shadow, the not-yet-seen, neglected or forgotten "periphery", which here can be seen as equivalent to the idea and reality of unconsciousness, as *the not-yet-speech-ripe*. Smith's words evoke a strong sense of the oft-mentioned effort in working with dreams to bring the known across the bridge to the unknown, and vice versa –the apparently mundane coming into concert with the sacred. Here the words are slightly different, "subliminal" (read *unconscious*) and "focal" (read *conscious*) awareness. And isn't "awareness" a word and an experience that can lead to consciousness?

In this way, we might begin and continue to learn how sound becomes a vehicle for opening up to the many-voiced levels of an endless array of vitally instructive experiences and realities. This path illustrates how certain receptions of sound are an echo of the kind of expansive and imaginative energies, which are to be encountered in our dreaming lives too.

Bringing these focal practices together may open us yet more deeply to the felt-sense wherein we may become aware of that which exists in the peripheries. Such involvement may enhance our experience of *the All-That-Is*, visible and invisible, physical and spiritual, alive and dead, felt and thought, sensed and intuited, as we walk on the many pathways of our existences awake and asleep, dreaming and exploring amid the known and unknown elements of our existences. We might perhaps find the sacred in the ordinary and the ordinary in the sacred through this practice as well. And lest we think or feel that "it's all about us", we may equally note that the energies and gifts of dreams and music are capable of serving the wild nature of this earth for the enrichment of the many lives and energies we view as other than our own, all her furry four-leggeds, winged ones, her green saplings, scaly swimmers, flowing rapids and billowing clouds, the mighty mountains, depth-renewing vales and stretching sand-filled deserts.

RESONANCE & THE DREAMING SONG OF THE LAND

When we listen to a piece of music, live or recorded, dream our dreams, and when we find ourselves in whatever atmosphere we happen to inhabit at a given moment, we resonate with our surroundings. A terrifying dream leaves us frightened, suggesting we were hosting a fear even before the dream knocked on our door. An energetic song gets us revved up. A walk on the beach, down a soulful city lane or in a natural setting like a park or wood clears our minds and recuperates the senses.

So far in this work, I've summoned the word *resonance* many times. We may intuitively or otherwise know what is meant by this word. Sound Healers, in particular, base our work upon this central principle of calling up sound for the pursuit of healing and seeking wholeness.

Resonance, in this sense, refers to the tendency of one form to fall into a fellow feeling with another. As we resonate, we resound an original cadence being made nearby, if not a cadence, then a melody, if not melody, then rhythm or silence. In reverberating with a peaceful sound, one becomes at peace, tranquil. To resonate with another form of being is to vibrate in response with it. So really, any sound, mood or atmosphere can and does encourage resonance.

Entrainment is yet another technical term used by Sound Healers, referring to a further level of resonance. In working with music and sound, it's possible to "entrain" brainwaves, tissues and water in the body to match or sync up with certain waves, or frequencies of sound. Gaynor speaks of the concept of entrainment as, " the process by which powerful rhythmic vibrations of one object are *projected* onto a second object with a similar frequency."

Aha! Sound can be understood to project outward from its source. In a very real way, then, the sending and receiving of sound also relates to psycho-spiritual projection – the projects of our lives. In both entrainment and resonance what is occurring is that a stronger, more alluring or desired frequency influences another person, being or listener in such a way that the consciousness, the attention and the matter in the body take on the projection, the frequency that is being sent out.

This is simply another way of understanding what may be obvious to us from our everyday experiences. Yet do we make all the connections that are possible here? When an ambulance on its way to a call drives down the street upon which we are standing or walking, the sound of its alarm affects and influences our very tissues. Of course, we recognize that an ambulance means an emergency and this may bring unpleasant or concerned thoughts to mind about the people involved in the crisis or past memories and feelings of our own emergencies. On the material level and even in the psyche, we become entrained to the very sounds that the siren is emitting as that alert-filled sound-aura affects all kinds of changes in our being, if even only for a few moments. The siren can be understood as filling one with a sense of alarm, in this case.

There are many examples of resonance and entrainment. To share another couple instances, and to perhaps heal from our imagined version of the emergency above, consider the sound of rushing or flowing water. When one is out in the wilderness, walking, visioning, camping, or even at home pouring a bath, it is natural to come into resonance with the tone of the surroundings. Imagine stopping for a rest near a mountainous stream, or turning on the hot water at the end of a long day for a soak in the tub. In such examples, from one very true perspective, what is taking place is that we are attuning ourselves to the actual frequencies of the elements. The energy and very humor of water shifts our mood and mode as a result of how the outer force of the river, the waterfall or the plumbing in the bath shift our very physiology and psyche through the reception of these flowing energies within the body, spirit and soul. The sound of water itself entrains the measurable waves in the brain – note that we use a metaphor of water itself to describe what appears to occur in the mind – and like a seasoned musician, the old grey matter picks up the rhythm "naturally" and begins to *flow* with the given composition.

It's also been shown how water takes on, or resonates with, the frequency of vibration happening nearby. Our bodies, just like the planet we inhabit, are composed of roughly 70% water. So, that same percentage takes on the "vibes" of whatever sounds – audible or not – are taking place in the surrounding environs. Very simply, you can see this when you gently bump or push a glass filled with water. The liquid within takes on the shape and energy of that movement. And so it does with sound, albeit on several more subtle levels.

If you live in the city and make forays into the park, country, or nature, or like to take walks in the woods, you know that there's a strong yet settling quality that becalms one when entering such places. This has happened to me many times over my life. Often, when I first leave the urban domain of metropolis I will begin to feel relaxed and even sleepy as a result. This is resonance and entrainment in action. The cornucopia of healing sights, sounds and realities to be found in non-technologized settings, are experienced as such, in large part due to the fact that they inhere a holistic natural frequency of sound, being and belonging that is often, but not always, less intense and driven than the pace to be found in any modern city.

When we simply pay deep attention to our immediate experience we may not require such theoretical or conceptual frameworks. In a way these ideas are truly helpful and shed a kind of new light, yet such truths have been clear to indigenous, archaic and traditional peoples for thousands of years. It's like the old saying that "music is the solace that soothes the savage beast". Anyone who has listened closely to a Miles Davis album or a Loreena McKennit concert, and many other kinds of music, knows that their effects are real and carry the ability to influence felt-experience.

OUR PROJECTS CREATE
RESONANCE AND ENTRAINMENT

We see that sound creates profound designs. We may also be able to consider how other energetic forms, such as dreams and projections, determine or reveal qualities of experience. Equally, the way we feel and think and imagine has an influence towards all the living beings that we share this earth with, as well as the very ground upon which we tread. They could inform our being too.

Shamans, soul doctors and the holy people of old, as well as more recently, have used music and sound to bless and call the very elements, to imbue, honor, come into tune with and respect the weather and for finding personal and cultural forms of efficacious healing, as we've discussed elsewhere in this book.

Here, I'd like to further shore up that one of the ways we can honor our dreams, the otherworlds, the dreams of our lives and the dream of the living world which houses us so graciously as humans, is to make holy kinds of sacred sound and music for our selves, each other, the plant people, the animals, the stones and fields, the waving grasses awash in the wind-filled skies and even the small yet equally significant insect beings we cohabitate with in this mesocosm we call "Earth".

In this pursuit, there's heft of a helpful variety to how storyteller Martin Shaw describes his understanding of the mythic. Shaw beseeches us to consider that myth is really the *dreaming of place*: the living, visionary, story and song-infused, containing, rupturing, blessed lore of the land, creatures and very places we find ourselves living and dying amongst. This includes for unexpected locales such as cities, which are built-up yet also can be soulful domains that equally rest upon the ever-living and ever-dying, greening and brown-turning earth. Remember the etymology for the word "dream"? Please consider now that the story of this word accounts also for the second half of its origins as *a joyful noise*. To be fair and round and whole, recall that the first half of the old meaning of dream is *a deceptive phantasm*.

It's probably true that each of us could perceive one or the other of these, a nightmare and/or a beauteous song, in any place on the planet if we spent enough time there. All places upon and within the achingly beautiful earth embody and besitr shadows and celebrations. It's also the case that dreams are more than the word etymology suggests. Equally true, in my experience and in that of many people I work with and respect deeply, is that even when it comes to Nature, it's possible for us to project ideas, values and feelings outside ourselves and upon the animals and growing things as well as the landscapes we encounter in and along our many travels.

Some may see a storm as a boon while others may see it as a curse. Or consider an old trickster. Some folks may come upon a coyote in the wild, at home or in a dream and consider it an unwholesome danger. Others will perhaps find such an encounter a blessing. Still others may even try to allow the coyote to be who it is and to attempt to know and understand this creature for how it appears, and may see both at the same time, a bestowing gift, a potential terror, and another one of creations paradoxical living people who serves many purposes in a divinely intersecting web of life and death; to study and learn from coyote's qualities, personality and characteristics may be the most endearing approach. Even though our projections hold meaning, it doesn't mean that they hold or necessarily reflect the only word on the matter.

From a wider view, swirling storms, yelping coyotes, swarming insects, mountains on high with jutting jagged edges, breath-taking vistas, sweeping valleys below cradling calm meadows and tranquil, heady aromas are not distinct or separate forces that are necessarily to be categorized. All creatures and earthscapes, all weather and growing, seeding, dying back and returning life on the earth has its own dream, and we all may see that existence occurs within a much bigger dream than that which we are usually aware of, the one that we call Life, Existence, Death and Rebirth, or, call it The Great Cosmic Story on the Road of Life and Death, if you like.

If what Shaw is proposing is true (and I think he's really onto something), then in a very real sense, myth as the dreaming-story of place is equally also a public *and* a private affair.

Another thread that has been dovetailing in and out during the course of our journey here has been the fibrous weaving that displays how ancient, traditional and intact people have known these notions in their own way, for a very long time. How might sound and music fit with all of this in an ancient and eternal sense that we might come to reconsider now, in our time?

Considering dreams related to sound, as *a joyful noise*, a heard image issuing forth within the organ of the imagination, let's cast our attention towards an observation from author Bruce Chatwin who spent time with Aboriginal Australians and wrote a book about his gleanings called *The Songlines*,

> "In Aboriginal belief an unsung land is a dead land: since, if the songs are forgotten, the land itself will die."[5]

Chatwin describes how some of the oldest known people on earth not only navigate and orient through singing songs to and of the very land, they also have used music to feed and keep alive the very earth beneath their feet. The songs themselves tell stories of the people, land, divinities, animals and elements, recounting origins as witnessed and related within a dreaming, mystical-yet-embodied, awake everyday awareness. The songlines are like a living, sounding and breathing mythos that also helps to "keep the dream alive". Music-making of this sort becomes a practical yet also beguiling, fulsome offering to the land and her living people. To my mind and heart, this is another level of *the dream of the earth*, the myth of the land, the collective visionary reality that we can re-inhabit, each one of us today, no matter where we live and no matter in how small or large a fashion.

We live in a time when this deep respect and resonantly soulful practice for acknowledging life, death and existence as they actually already are, appears to be most needed by all the energies and beings of the earth and is perhaps also longed for by the very Cosmos which we dwell within. Yet, just as with our discussion about working with sound and dreams, we would do well to first listen and pay attention and seek to receive and give space to the myths, dreams and stories of the places we cohabitate. What are the needs and the stories, the dreams, the personalities of the lands, creatures, oceans and skies? What are the longings and truths of the birds in the forest, the fish in the rivers and the seas? What might clouds desire and evoke, or stars in the nighttime sky far above them? What ravishment might the moon herself request and bequeath? What are *their* stories and how might we show them that we are willing to return the vast wealth of gifts we are given by these living, mighty and vibrantly aware forces, which we depend upon for our very sustenance for being able to wake up in the morning?

If we can respectfully, that is to say *reflectively*, see and feel our place in their mythologies and their dreaming domains, we might be capable of crafting simple or complex songs, utterances,

stories and poems that could care for all of these elements and
forces the way they so dutifully and unreasonably care about and
sing for us. Such artful stirrings could also underpin the pragmatic
creative necessities of architecture and the crafting of soulful
infrastructures in our cities that might go with, rather than against
the primordial designs of the wild..

In this way, we might be found living within mythos
ourselves, singing the unsung land back to life, jumping, laughing,
dancing and weeping, rolling, waltzing, laying on our backs in the
wilding grasses, sheltering within escarpments nestled in rocky
enclaves watching storm-laden divinities pass before our very eyes
as lightning flashes and thunder peels across the heavens.

If we live in the city, maybe we will sing to the very walls
and glass windows of our homes and offices, sending a parlez of
soulful resonance to the sidewalks and labyrinthine streets of the
metropolis. Why not sing the praises of our houseplants, the
devoted furniture and the ever-serviceable roofs over our heads?
All good floors enjoy the weight of a pulsating jig and a heartfelt,
stomped-out rhythm. So I'm told, by my own well-worn, soiled,
foot-filled and toe-kissed home. When the birds arrive at the break
of dawn, or in the gloamy evening, why not accompany them with
a spontaneous tune of thanks for the sufficiency and unexpected
providence or difficult challenges of the day and the secreted

messages telling of spirit that they bring from afar amid their own constant travails?

Wherever we find ourselves living, we may give voice to the dreams of our lives and the lives of our dreams through a humble, close to the ground, at times lofty and soaring, mighty effort to sing the dreams, the mythic lore of the places we could find ourselves belonging to on this road of life and death. It will take some serious ability to listen to the dreaming songs of all that lives around and outside of us too. In so doing, we consider the needs and living-dying qualities of the forces that nestle us and care for us. We may also honor the beauty and living grace of a deep dreaming intelligence that dwells within each of us when we understand that the Dream of Life is also connected to the Great Song and the Mythos of Place. Each of these may be seen and felt to also be fed and held up by the Dream of Death, the Songs of Dying and the unending Rhythm of the Dance of Life-Death-Life that supports and is woven into all that we call Existence.

Endnotes Chapter 7

[1] R.J. Stewart, "The Spiritual Dimensions of Music", 1990, Destiny Books, Rochester, Vermont, p.46

[2] Monika Wikman, "Pregnant Darkness"

[3] Mandawuy Yunupingu, from the Foreword to Karl Neuenfeldt's "The Didjeridu from Arnhem Land to Internet", 1997, John Libby, Perfect Beat Publications, p.xiii

[4] Mitchell L. Gaynor, (quoting Huston Smith in the film, "Requiem for a Faith), "The Healing Power of Sound, Recovering from Life-Threatening Illness Using Sound, Voice and Music", 1999, Shambala Publications, London, p. 45-46

[5] Bruce Chatwin, "The Songlines", 1988, Penguin Books, p.52

CHAPTER 8

Ancient and Contemporary Dream Incubation

"Steadiness is essential. Forwards... or backwards we will not look. Let us learn to live swaying, in a rocking boat on the sea."
Friedrich Holderlin

In much of the contemporary literature on dream work, you'll find helpful practices for how to seek answers and guidance while asleep and dreaming. Such exercises are often referred to as *incubation.* The basic idea of these protocols is to form a question to pose to the energies, people, situations and sources of dreams. The dreamer does this before going to sleep, perhaps writing the query down in one's journal or on a note tucked under the pillow. She or he then reviews the recalled dreams after awakening, looking for clues and answers to the dream question. I've tried this technique, recommended it to others and it works. However, the resulting dream doesn't always yield up immediately easy to understand or clearly connected responses. Dreams are usually more mysterious, playful, adept and bigger than that. Almost always, in my experience, the dreams do clearly provide a helpful response, albeit in language that tends not to be readily understandable to the solo dreamer working with dream material alone. In many cases too, we might not get the response we *think* we need or want.

I find that when I pose questions to dreams, they do provide "answers", yet the dreaming source's purposes tend to be much more encompassing than waking ambitions. And so, often one may be expecting some dream advice that the waking self feels would be of benefit. In my experience, the dreams always address what the Deep Self and the divinities that appear to craft them deem to be the most fruitful, in terms of continuously creating and unveiling experiences that serve wholeness, versus one's own limited ideas about what seems to be called for in the dayworld of action, "progress" and achievement. The dreams offer up perspectives for focusing on that which needs to be dealt with as regards being and belonging versus only addressing action plans that the ego may be desiring for the surreptitious gaining of one more layer of elusive yet hoped for security, accomplishment or power. The dreams also seek to address "all of the above", at the same time, and speak to the need for action, empowerment and achievement, as well.

There are several ancient traditions related to dream incubation that we can study and learn about which I have found helpful, soul-stirring and intriguing. These point to a slightly different way of growing and hatching wholeness-bound, holy (full of holes!) visions. Myself, and many others have found it instructive and emboldening to relate with these historical taproots of ancestral practices and old disciplines. By exploring such traditions, it is possible to create new ones, to build upon and honor what has come before. By reviewing these timeless disciplines, we probably don't want to mimic them. The point is not to attempt to live in the past, or try to go back to a more idyllic time. This doesn't seem possible, in any case, to my mind and heart. Rather, by honoring and studying the long ago, we learn what we are able to cull from the past and bring these ideas and realities forward for ourselves, and each other, in the present and for the future. Our undertakings may also aid us in acknowledging the wealth of earlier dreamers' engagements with vital forms of apparent wisdom that seem to be missing in today's world in so many ways. This path can be a way to honor and feed the past and sup a taste of the eternal too.

ANCIENT GREEK DREAM WORK & ASKLEPIOS

It's apparently true that there's something inherently timeless about certain human enterprises and connected sacred energies. Peter Kingsley has written enthrallingly about dream incubation in the 4th and 5th centuries, carried out by archaic Greek poets, mystics, lovers of wisdom and healers. Kingsley's work artfully shows us throughout the pages of his book *In the Dark Places of Wisdom* how certain trance-inducing dream journeys formed the core of a very old yet perceivably timeless culture-spring,

> "Healers known as Iatromantis... for them the prophecy was what came first – the ability to look behind the scenes, see what others don't. The healing followed as a matter of course... They were famous for their use of incantations: for chanting or repeating words in a way that can seem awkward or senseless but that has a certain effect, is able to induce a change in someone who says or hears them. And they used techniques of breath control to help break the hold of the senses, create access to an awareness beyond space and time... Their knowledge was entirely different from what knowledge is to us. And they got it from incubation."[1]

This original source of vibrant and alive spiritual knowledge has slowly been covered over in favor of what we have come to recognize as the legacy of rationalistic-materialist intellectualism. From Kingsley's incantational, insightful writing, an unexpected past emerges. Here we witness rites of passage, wherein incubatory dream healings shape the basis of what could accurately be compared with certain Buddhist meditation practices, Shamanistic healing arts, contemporary and ancient Breath Work modalities, that all bear a relation to the old incubatory disciplines. Such associations reveal an ancient Greek heritage of profound mystical yet practical proportions. In this custom, as I understand it, dreams would be received during the actual incubation, while semi-awake, versus while the dreamer was fully asleep.

In the picture Kingsley paints so adeptly, the ancient predecessors of western civilization were actually a people who centrally engaged in a dream journey art, through which they encountered the energies and presences of other worlds, as a basis for orienting culture in relation to spirit and soul within this so-called middle world we inhabit as humans. Kingsley's well-evinced researches show how this past dreaming culture was composed of, at heart, intrepid mystical seekers. These dreamers appear to have engaged in incubation for practicable purposes of learning through directly pragmatic, though equally mystical experience. This antique discipline allowed for the bringing back of boons, which served to help create the culture, which became part of everyday human life, imbued by the numinous, mysterious-spiritual-soulful quality of dreams and visionary states.

While reading *In the Dark Places of Wisdom* and *Reality* - two of Kingsley's works on this topic - one sees how all the elements that have been associated with Asklepian Dream Healing throughout the Mediterranean were actually present earlier than was previously thought. Apparently incubation, as the ancient Greeks knew it, had been taught and practiced under the auspices and influence of the god whom medical doctors pay allegiance to even today. We know him by the moniker *Apollo*.

Per Kingsley, prior to the rise of the Athenian empire and the reign of Plato and Aristotle, Apollo himself was experienced as a much more mysterious and enigmatic archetypal presence than we have been led to believe he might be. The assignment of Apollo as "the God of Reason" appears to have come later, as the result of certain projections based upon a human lopsidedness, which sought to banish ambiguity and darkness, stillness and nonsensical wisdom. Perhaps such a predicament sounds familiar to us, in our time? Apollo, mytho-historically, is said to be the father of Asklepios, the half-human, half-divine figure associated with Greek dream incubation and healing.

Asklepios is a fitting mediator between the Other World and this one in his half-mortal, half-divine archetypical origins. We might do well to note that Jesus holds similar associations as the son of God and a mortal woman. Asklepios' mother, too, was human and his father was a god. In a very palpable sense, this gives the god of dream healing a role intrinsically predisposed to mediating imaginal reality between the divine and the human. Asklepios is a bridge-walker, a presence capable of tending the reality of this world and the dreaming, spirit worlds.

PHILOSOPHY, THE ANCIENT LOVE OF WISDOM

The resurfacing today of what was known and practiced by the old ones in relation to incubation is no accident. Inscriptions on old tablets and the poetry of Parmeneides, in addition to a growing wealth of knowledge about the Asklepian practices, add up to reveal a mystifyingly beautiful, yet also life-serving, well-grounded picture of a potent spiritual-visionary inheritance.

Parmeneides was a well-known ancient Greek philosopher and poet who drew knowledge and learning from the old practice of philosophy as *the love of wisdom*. These are the roots of the word *philosophy* itself, as reflected in its origins; "philo", meaning *love* and "sophia", *wisdom*. This old understanding of and appreciation for a native, alive intelligence is connected with how journeying into the imagination - the place where images arise and live - is and has been a vital source of psycho-spiritual, physical healing and wholeness, woven into the fabric of western life for thousands of years.

Buried within the covered over soils of this aged practice, and amongst the twining ancestral fibers of the Western World, lie the paradoxical seeds of a richly returned harvest of dreaming arts. This rediscovery can reveal to us a central bequeathing, from which we may contemporarily revitalize our own experience by making deeply transformative dream journeys in a similar fashion. In remembering our capacity to dream in semi-waking states and asleep through incubation, we may also learn to dream with and for one another, the breathing land, the swirling waters, the wily weather, the wild animals of the earth, the ever-greening plants and sprouts of the flora kingdom as well as with the feathered creatures of the air. We could also learn a thing or two about destruction, death and rebirth.

In antiquity, incubatory dream travelers created temples, dream caves, wombs in the terra firma, entryways into *the world under and behind the world*, portals to other realities. Later came the abatons of Asklepios, which can still be visited today in certain parts of Greece, Turkey and Italy. Abatons are constructed, womb-like dreaming chambers inside the old temples, where the ancient vision-seekers would go to meet healing visions and to dream.

How might we further honor, learn from and celebrate our dreams for the receiving and honing of wisdom today? Where are *our* dream temples, the sacred cave wombs and hunting grounds for relating to and feeding the guiding voices of the Dreamtime?

IMAGINATION AND SOUND IN ANCIENT INCUBATION

Practitioners of archaic dream healing gained assistance from previously initiated technicians of the incubatory path, dream priests – an ancient type of dream worker. These priests were apparently much like mentors, who helped others connect with dreams for the gaining of direct, immediate, imaginal experience.

The old art was a practice for becoming totally still in a dark place, as Kingsley puts it, "like an animal". Dreamers would imbibe visions in this state following abstinence from food and drink and also often after performing ritual baths of purification in nearby springs or natural water sources. Remember the way the young daughter was cast into the ocean? Something deep, fluid and true ties the energies of water, wisdom and dreaming together.

Ancient incubatory experience involved a state of being *half-awake* and *half-asleep*. Such a form of 'semi-consciousness' allows for a more awakened experience of the dreaming energies. In the old ways of practicing incubation, while dreaming, one opened up to and witnessed telltale hallmarks of initiatory experience, such as the sound of a hissing snake. This sensation is similar to what has been reported widely in connection to the Kundalini Rising phenomenon – the activation of the mythic-energetic serpent at the base of the spine. Tree snakes were present at the temples in the old rites as an aid to embodying dreaming visions and also were beheld as representatives of the god of dream healing, Asklepios, who also works with a dog helper.

The hissing of snakes, as heard by these dream seekers, suggests the mystery of sound as it relates to healing, the access to certain modes of consciousness through accompanying aural elements. This hissing took a later form of musical and ritual theatre as played out in the Asklepian temples, where the temple snakes found homes and would sometimes also slither alongside those seeking dreams during their incubatory, healing journeys in the abatons.

Jeanne Actherberg writes in her book on shamanic states of wholeness, *Imagery in Healing, Shamanism and Modern Medicine*:

"Moving from patient to patient, the group (of ancient healers) carried the accoutrements of the physician... medicines and surgical tools, and performed... both the standard medical treatments as well as magical rites. In the semidarkness, in the presence of the earthly representatives of healing deities, with music playing in the background, and surrounded by all the pomp and circumstance of the magnificent shrines, whatever innate healing ability the patients possessed in the face of their grave illnesses was greatly enhanced. It was a perfect situation for the imagination to go to work ..." [2]

It is largely considered that other ancient cultures have maintained similar engagements to those described above, with the imagination, the realms of the spirits and the Dreaming, in their own incubation practices. Some scholars feel confident that incubation existed in early Egyptian culture and that this prior tradition would have influenced the Greeks. It has been shown that much of Greek culture was a re-enculturation of earlier modes from the Egyptian peoples of the past who dwelt across the sea.

In that even more ancient land and culture, the divinity associated with incubation would have been Imhotep, considered a forerunner of Asklepios. I have enjoyed my own first-hand experiences of this energy in Egypt, having performed a number of contemporary dream and sound healing ceremonies there on three consecutive annual sojourns to that bewildering and enchanting country.

All up and down the Nile River, in the olden temple complexes of one of the most enigmatic original cultures on the planet, from Cairo to Philae, I have had the pleasure of leading sound healing and dream meditations for groups of travelers seeking forms of spiritual and soul remembrance. From what I've witnessed and learned while doing so, it seems clear that old-time Egyptians must have been using music and sound as powerful tools for engaging in dream-hatching incubatory experiences.

It's equally apparent that the Egyptians had their own versions of shamanistic practices expressing the actual and symbolic energies of death and transformation, the Life-Death-Life cycle we discussed in connection with the tale of Skeleton Woman in an earlier chapter. The conception surrounding the journey into the so-called "afterlife" of the Pharaoh, for example, apparently involved being entombed in a sarcophagus, which then became the container for a spiritual rebirth and renewal into the Beyond. Such a notion is corroborated by mythological evidence to be found elaborated in various hieroglyphic texts that have been studied and written about by several authors. Von Franz details the symbolic roots of these motifs in ancient Egypt in her book, *Alchemy*.

A dream ritual I have provided sound and structure for is one in which our group has gathered amid silence and the careful shuffling of feet in the King's Chamber of the Great Pyramid in Giza, where an elemental marble coffin still rises up out of the stone-hewn floor. In this waking incubatory dream journey ceremony, I have played Native American Flutes, and the Aboriginal Australian Didjeridu for participants as they lay surrendered in the Pharaoh's coffin. In this creative contemporary rite, we each enacted our own version of a symbolic death-rebirth experience. The acoustics in this space are incredible, and swell with a reverberation that builds upon itself as it enigmatically drifts off into other dimensions, connecting the body and the physical space to the spirit ethers within, surrounding and beyond fully physical earthly forms.

Gayle Delaney has laid out some very interesting research related to this, done by Norman MacKenzie, author of *Dreams and Dreaming*. She quotes MacKenzie in her book *All About Dreams:*

> "The priests at Memphis, like those in the sanctuary of Isis at Philae, and at the oracles of Khimunu and Thebes, practiced incubation... sick persons were brought to sleep in the temple, where they fasted, or took potions, to induce beneficial dreams."[3]

When one considers that cultures throughout time have made use of music to open to the energies of the spirits and other realms, it's not unlikely that the Egyptians had their own version. Researchers, scholars and explorers are still uncovering more about the use of music in ancient ceremonies and rituals in Egypt to this very day.

Perhaps of great interest to people of Celtic and Anglo descent, is the evident history of dream incubation practices in ancient Ireland and Britain, which has been made quite clear by lauded expert on Celtic traditions, John Matthews. Due to the prolific quality of the ancient Celts who made their way throughout Europe and elsewhere, it is very likely that several Western peoples alive today have some ancestral roots of blood tie with Celtic and related peoples. Such connections strongly imply archetypal threads that weave through the fabric of time and bear some relation to a felt psychic memory within many around the existence and viability of these olden practices.

Matthews writes about remnants of dream incubation, as it exists in the mythos and stories of the Celts and also the physical clues of a suspected dream temple in Gloucestershire at Lydney. This locale offers remnants depicting the worship of a dream god named Nodens, who is similar to Asklepios in many ways. The resemblance includes the endearing detail of the fact that Nodens, like Asklepios worked dream healings with the assistance of a psychopomp canine ally. Nodens is also thought to bear resemblance to the Greek figure of Phoebus Apollo and also Neptune. This is due to the apparent fact that the god used a chariot drawn by four horses, in addition to the import of water, as connected to his deified character and reflected in records found at Lydney.

The similarities in ancient Celtic dream culture with the old Greek temples and abatons, as well as a parallel of praxis, is referred to in Matthews' book about Irish Poet, Shaman and Seer, Taliesen,

> "The temple itself bears a remarkable resemblance to the Asklepion at Epidauros in Greece, where a kind of healing ritual known as 'incubation' was practiced. In this the sufferers, having first sacrificed to the god of the place, then entered a special bath house and, after purifying themselves, were taken to a building which contained a number of small cubicles. There the subject slept and, if the god willed it, received a dream which conveyed to them the means by which they were to be healed."[4]

Such ancient practices suggest a form of forgotten, yet able to be remembered spiritual inheritance. The revived interest in these disciplines may be understood as arising out of the energetic and archetypal influence of the ancestors and dream healing divinities via the world soul, objective psyche or the collective unconscious. In other words, continued interest, and in some cases even symbolic representations of such activity in dreams themselves, strongly imply that this practice is one that lives in the very marrow of our bones and the wellspring of the true imagination. I've also experienced that these incubatory energies come forth out of the living fabrics of the soil and issue from the mouths of the plant and animal people when their voice is attended to.

Matthews has more to say in his practical skills guidebook *The Celtic Shaman* where he also describes in detail an exercise for contemporary incubation,

> "Another method of healing practiced among the Celts (as in many other parts of the world) was that of incubation. Here the sufferer, after being suitably prepared, slept in a special hut or cave, and there incubated a dream in which he or she either received a visitation from one of the gods of healing, or was instructed in a form of self-cure – often cryptically, or in a form requiring interpretation… That some form of incubatory sleep was practiced among the Celts is well attested…"[5]

So we can see that across cultures and in various places through time there have existed modes of dream healing, which suggest deeply related forms of dream seeking and also bear some profound relevance to those of us alive today who are curious to learn more about how to vitally work with and learn from our dreams.

MUSICAL INCUBATION
IN CONTEMPORARY SETTINGS

In considering the ancient practices, it becomes possible to learn something that can be invoked now. Although the trappings of culture and certain important elements of our lives evolve and change (and by "evolve", I mean "unfold", close to the original meaning of the word itself), there are threads of eternity that run across and throughout time and connect us to our ancestors through the ages. As Carl Jung put it during a Dream Seminar that has been published as part of the Bollingen Series under the title *Dream Analysis*,

> "Those ideas that have been alive through the centuries are most likely to return and to be operative. They are archetypes, the historical way of functioning, and so the general way."[6]

And Martin Shaw has also said,

"The prophetic seeks not to destroy old forms but rather to reanimate their propensity for holy thought".

The primal experience of what it means and feels like to watch the sun as it crests the enormous curve of the earth in the morning, for instance, is the kind of experience that has changed very little for us over thousands of years. From a human, soul-infused perspective there's a timeworn resonance with that blazing orb in the center of the galaxy, which induces a sense of such enormous force that it practically appears to be endless. The rising sun is like a poem from the Divine telling us that life may continue for one more day across the wide span of the incredible Earth. These days, as many now may be doing, we could also ask ourselves, "What would happen if we fell out of favor with that mighty energy"?

In our dreams, several timeless connections also weave in and out, suggesting lasting communion with people, places, beings and situations, who have come before us, who are here now and with those who will follow. This legacy is more than genetic, not merely "scientific" truth. Dreams tell of mythical beings and elemental forces, that have been spoken of and written about through time amid diverse peoples and cultures. This observable phenomenon demands our attention when we dream of forces that we can locate in the mythological traditions of our predecessors, as well as in each other's dreaming travels in the present. So very often, mythic situations and personages appear in our dreams, which we can see upon close examination are not realities that we've as yet encountered in waking circumstances in this lifetime. My partner of twelve years recently dreamed that she turned into Garuda, the ancient mythical eagle of East Indian mythos. As far as she knows, she tells me, she's never studied, read or previously considered this sacred animal personage before. Such occurrences give weight to the notion that in dreams we are open to the vast fabrics of an ancestral memory that goes beyond this actual physical lifetime. Yet these powers also, gratefully, include and are knowable within the context of the very days and nights that cradle us now.

A deep interest in these old ways has been teased out along my own treading of the byways running through complimentary studies of dreaming and music. Before I ever began to research ancient forms of incubation, I found myself offering musical meditations in dreaming circles and workshops as a portal of opening to the remembrance of nighttime dreams as well as for calling upon the guidance of in-the-moment healing visions.

Playing instruments such as the Aboriginal Australian Didjeridu, Tibetan Bowls, Native American Flutes and Drums, in a sacred space with willing dreamers and adventurers, has helped to co-create tremendously helpful dreams for myself and others, and, I trust, for blowing clouds and wending waterways, astute black-tailed deer and fleet-footed rabbits.

Sound truly *is an opener*. It releases us to the resonance of vibration that surrounds and permeates our physical forms, unveiling rich inner landscapes within the psyche, taking our awareness into and beyond familiar limits, creating connection with the spiritual and the everyday corners of the everyday we bump around in week to week.

In *the Bardo Thodol* or *Tibetan Book of the Dead*, Lama Govinda beautifully describes how sound, spirit and hearing are all connected,

> "the word listening (*thodol*, Tibetan for listening or hearing) in this connection, implies 'hearing with one's heart', that is, with sincere faith."[7]

For ages, people around the world have used music to call down the spirits, enter the heart more fully and find faith where none may seem to exist.

In the Tibetan Buddhist and older Bon traditions, the singing bowls used in meditation and ceremony are understood, along with certain chants, as the *sound of the Void*. Shamans from Siberia to North America have used the frame drum for opening portals to dreaming realities. Aboriginal folk in "The Land Down Under" have honored the didjeridu as a means for vibratory, spiritual, soul, community, individual and physical healing. The First People of Australia also use the didjeridu to assist the souls' transition during the act of dying. *Ten Canoes*, the first film about Aboriginal Australians that was made according to the people's own representation of their culture contains a beautiful rendition of this form of ceremonial. Native Americans have honored the spirits, as well as the elements of wood, earth, breath and wind, for many ages, in their use of the flute to perform ritual and courtship. Cultures around the world have drawn upon the human voice to effect and create healing energies with its' power to becalm and inspire mind, body, spirit, heart and soul, to express, live and evoke grief, and for connecting with the divine energies of so-called non-ordinary dreaming realities. All within the landscape of this earthy terrain of the world.

The way we carry the old incubations in a present-day mode is by gathering in a nourishing setting, where we know we can safely share and enter dreaming spaces together. In our meetings, dreamers are encouraged to lie down, close their eyes and to become, as Kingsley puts it "quite still, like animals". Further guidance is offered to pay attention to the imaginal, to follow the cycle of surrendered breathing and to notice the sensations in each one's own body. Often I will share a poem or a few words about the old rites of incubation as we begin. We co-create our very own dreaming temple abaton. When we do this, I suggest that by the mere act of collecting in this way to engage our dreams, we are in effect, co-creating a powerful visionary garment together. When we engage in sound healing incubation, I also ask participants to identify intentions for helpful, healing dreams, both within the time that the music is being offered, and also for the nights and days following the journey.

One woman reported a sleep dream in our circle the morning after one such incubation, which she felt was connected to the musical sound healing the night before. She said she didn't know what to make of it, but wanted to share her dream with our group and work with its' energies. We did, and found that the dream offered up excellent advice for the dreamer and the rest of us.

In particular, the work highlighted an answer to the question surrounding the dreamers' own intention of finding clarity about undergoing a major medical operation. The dream she shared seemed to verify going ahead with a surgery to remove fibroid tumors and also made clear the strong likelihood that it would be a success. This dreamer later had the surgery, regained her health and reports a much more satisfying level of wellbeing than she felt prior to the operation, especially in relation to the problems the tumors were creating. Years later, she says that she has also recognized ways that the dream and working with it, in addition to the actual life experience, have supported deep psycho-spiritual changes and growth, that have greatly affected her current direction in life in far-reaching ways.

DREAMS REFLECT INCUBATORY HEALING MOTIFS

Another dreamer, more recently, shared a similarly efficacious experience during a weekend gathering. She reported a vivid dream that involved her visiting an intimate love interest in a surreal setting in the dream world. In her dream, she discovered a man like one she knows in waking life, present within a setting she described as a kind of large cavernous void.

Here's her rendition of the experience…

In the dream, in a canoe-like boat, a man I'm involved with in waking life is under water, on the edge of drowning, with his face barely rising up above the surface, liquid coming in and

filling the hull of the craft. Around the edges of the canoe, space
appears to spill out and down into a brightly lit abyss. I know he is
suffering from the life-threatening illness he is dealing with in
waking life. As I realize this, I make the choice to breathe new life
into him through the act of leaning down and placing my lips on
his. This act appears to shift the energy in the dream so that we
next find ourselves in a well-trimmed, Victorian-era garden.

This dream evokes certain elements of archetypal, incubatory, healing energies that we could say were clearly brought about through the musical ceremony, which was performed the evening before the dream was recalled and then shared.

The tone, on one important level in the dream, of the man within (as represented by the intimate love interest from waking life) being in peril and in need of healing elicits several intriguing details held within the visions symbolic content. The magical-mysterious quality of the setting – a kind of dream void (akin to the King's Chamber in the Great Pyramids or a Grecian incubation abaton!) – wherein the vessel appears as a version of the boat that ferries souls into the Otherworld is stunning. The dream canoe is also like a version of the Egyptian sarcophagus, the transforming container wherein the physical form is placed, as part of a ceremonial act, supporting rebirth after the human body is no longer animated.

The reality of *dream death* is also evident here, further implying the energies, present in mythology and initiatory practices around the world and through time, of symbolic death and transformation. The way the dreamer seeks to heal the ill and near-to-dying man in the dream evokes the essential quality and character of the ancient dream incubations. Her response embodies the depth of a potent healing act, which springs from the heart and care of love and involves the energies of the spirit realms, the energies that exist beyond yet within literal physical domains of waking life. Notice the resemblance to the healing scene in the Skeleton Woman story.

This scenario in the dream also reveals the energy of *the willing sacrifice*. The dreamer knows the man has a communicable and terminal disease – in the dream as well as in waking life – and offers him the healing kiss, despite the perceived and understood risk to herself. When she makes this daring and compassionate choice, a garden appears and the energy of new growth and the greening of new life enter the experiential dream narrative.

In Egyptian mythology, when we amplify the dream material further, we find the essential energetic threads of the story of Isis resurrecting Osiris. Osiris is the ancient vegetative deity of the underworld, who parallels Dionysus (and Asklepios) in Greece and Jesus in the Christian tradition. This is the archetypal embodiment of the one who dies and is reborn, albeit in a new form and with a new identity, who is thereby able to renew the very land itself with green and shining tendrils of recreating, ever-birthing-and-dying plant beings.

Osiris' brother Set fooled him into entering a coffin at a social gathering, and killed the god, cutting his body up into pieces. He then spread his flesh across the land in an effort to dissipate his powers and influence. Isis later went and recollected Osiris' body and put him back together. Through this initiatory, dismembering passage, which resembles shamanic rites as well as a bevy of other mythic tales, Osiris eventually became the lord of the underworld through undergoing these trials and tribulations. As a consequence, it is his eloquence that sends the vital green shoots of new growth up out of the earth. Osiris is understood to be a renewing deity, in charge of the death and rebirth of the people, land, animals and plants upon and within the terrestrial plane, yet enlivened and transformed by the world behind and beneath the visible dayworld as we know it.

In the dream, this story plays itself out amid the personal though shared layers of the dreamers psyche. The over-riding flavors of initiation, the summons into trial leading to an ordeal and an assisted return, depict the mythic, psycho-spiritual cycle of renewal. The dreamer goes from the canoe/void/kiss scene to the garden, evoking a death and rebirth enactment.

The numinous, sacred qualities of this dream can be seen and understood as portions in the fabric of ancient cultures that also practiced and honored musical dream incubation and spiritual ceremony the way we did in our dream circle. By enjoining these energies through intentional practice, the timeless patterns of the deep psyche are experienced in the present moment, with potentially eternal yet specifically time-bound boons to offer the dreamer and the group participants.

Such experiences suggest that there is great healing and resonance to be found in bringing ceremony and sound to the engagements with our dreams. Through artful and sensuous-intuitive practices played out in our work, along with the feeling-thinking elements of the discussion-based and projective approach, a further level of healing, soul, humanity and depth is served.

These ancient, wholeness-creating energies are only so far away as our own willingness to engage the dreams with all of who we may find ourselves to be. Co-creating artful practices, such as musical incubation meditations and ceremonies, is one more way to express a willingness to participate in well-rounded fashions with the vital energies of the dream world.

Archetypal energies go beyond mere fascination and images. Jung wrote and spoke about this in the final chapter of one of the, perhaps, most accessible presentations from him on Analytical psychology (which includes contributions from many of the phenomenal female collaborators who worked with Jung), *Man and His Symbols*. One of the key aspects of archetypes is their emotionality. As Jung expresses, we want to be careful not to overlook the emotional side of our encounters with the energies of our dreams, lives, psyches, and in our explorations of myth. I would agree heartily with this and also add that in bringing music and sound to this work, emotion is granted a widened and deepened space of belonging, along with its deeper cousin, feeling.

DREAMS AND INCUBATION, PRACTICA FOR OUR AGE

The motifs that appear in the dream example described above evoke the very creative-destructive, sacrificial and transformative energies that have been related with in the past which could be most helpful to those of us alive today who would seek to find practical tools and viewpoints for imaginatively and favorably maneuvering through the emotionally, physically and spiritually challenging landscapes of our everyday lives.

I believe the dream above does an expert service by placing the dreamer and her ill love interest in a Victorian garden following the "saving kiss". Collectively and historically speaking, this was a moment when western civilization fully began to turn its backs on the mythic and imaginative folkloric traditions in favor of the materialist-scientific, rational standpoint. This is a way the dream has of speaking far beyond the exclusively personal level of meaning and it does so by pointing to where the energies of engaging truthfulness around imagination and the Life-Death-Life cycle may be reclaimed. In effect, the dream says, in order to go forward, we have to go back – to heal, we must go through.

In a related vein, as previously noted, we live in an era during which most folks can tend to think about and experience life in terms of the archetype of *apocalypsis*. The end of the world is a consideration on many minds and in many hearts in this age. It's been said that part of the issue plaguing modernity has to do with our perpetual tendency to view our lives and life on the planet in a mistakenly literal fashion. It seems extremely odd to me that, at a time when so many are conceiving of the "ultimate end" of everyone, we can also see how, at least in the West (America and Europe), multitudes of people seem unwilling to die.

On the one hand, there's a fear of the death of great numbers of people, and on the other, our medical and scientific technology continues to seek and promote longer and longer lives.

Long life, in terms of greater lifespan, doesn't necessarily equate with a well-lived life.

The original author, John of Patmos, who is said to have written the book of the Bible known as Revelations, which is widely accepted by some Christians as a prophetic description of "The End Times", was himself gripped by the archetypal, energetic and emotional sense of the endings of things. Penned nearly two thousand years ago, Patmos' vision was one that described his own and many people's feeling that the world was about to end at that time as well. Ironically and interestingly, here we are today looking back and pondering these very issues ourselves.

This is not to say that the matters of our day, and of past days, are not, or have not been serious and worthy of our best efforts, concerns and attentions. Rather, when we seriously study mythology and our dreams, asking vital questions about what might be true, allowing ourselves to be informed by the worlds within and without, we may recognize that there is something inherent about existence that always has us suspecting that everything is about to end. The archetype of apocalypse is paradoxically part of the fabric of the ongoing garment of life and death that the Divine perpetually reweaves along with our assistance.

This collaboration takes place knowingly and unknowingly, in our hearts and minds. Every end may be seen to lead to another beginning. Yet unless we cultivate the sense of this deeper truth of the living force of symbolic and actual reality, we mistakenly literalize our world and our experiences and continue to create unnecessarily tragic endings that are ultimately more painful than they may need to be through a mass ignorance of the very kinds of death-rebirth energies that metaphorically and actually appear in our dreams every night as we sleep as well as in our mythic storytelling traditions. These symbolic and imaginal visitations invite us to recognize ways of creatively refashioning the projects of our lives and deaths amid the dreams we live while awake.

When I say *death and rebirth*, I want to be clear that experiencing such energies in the soul or psyche does not immediately or realistically translate into an ability to know our actual deaths when they arrive. For, how can we truly know that experience fully until we find ourselves in it, engaged by our dying time? There are some difficult questions and distinctions to be made around all this that relate to the on-going mysteries of our days, the apparent end and spiritual continuation of them. We often say that we will know what it's like to die, because we've gone through certain kinds of death through the course of our days. Maybe, just maybe, we do have a taste of that. Still, the actual move away from inhabiting this body as it ceases to exist would rightly appear to be something one can only know through the experiencing of that active leap.

Perhaps the psychological undergoing of death, as symbolically witnessed in our dreams, might more accurately be called a change in forms, or transformation. It all raises a lot of questions, and we've grown so familiar with thinking that we really know what death involves. However, through the work of Stephen Jenkinson and his Orphan Wisdom School, as well as his, extremely important book *Die Wise*, I've begun to reconsider many of the taken-for-granted assumptions around these ideas and related realities. Jenkinson, who worked for many years with the Dying (and says he was with approximately eight hundred folks who died while they were "terminally ill" during his palliative care career) reports "from the trenches" that over and over again he witnessed people being totally disoriented by the news of their immanent death and totally incapable of dying. He also intones that he most often watched as people did everything they could, in conjunction with the medical establishment, to go on living, even when it was apparent that death was at hand – all strong indicators that the actual end of our human, earthly lives is not something that we are really acquainted with by the time we find ourselves having to go through the undertaking. So it would seem that we might want to ask ourselves how real and true our notions of understanding and being friends with death actually are. This all connects with how we either do or don't hold mythic tools for such things.

I also have a hearty hunch that our imaginations make use of what we think of dying, as a mode for expressing change itself. We've looked at this notion already throughout these pages. Perhaps it's best if we consciously decide to question our ideas about death as they pertain to the veritable truth of the actual thing itself.

When so-called "nasty" forms of death appear in dreams, it seems to be the case, through experience, that part of the invitation is to enter into the suffering and grief that such trials tend to occasion. This could be a way of familiarizing our knowledge with a deeper curiosity about and even intelligence towards how to die when we actually get there, and also a means of carrying it now, with the full realization that it will come to pass. At the same time, it seems wise, and even crucial when we consider Jenkinson's observations, not to mistake our actual dying time with superficial attempts to enlist ideas about transformation as a vehicle for avoiding the death that will come to each of us and which we could witness all around us through the course of our days and nights.

In these contemporary times, youth and people of all ages wonder if life is even worth living and whether or not there will be a world left standing for coming generations to inherit from those who have come and gone before. Climate change, pollution, war, mass killing and terrorism, ongoing racial and gender tensions, as well as species extinction, create literal and symbolic oceans of depression, confusion and trauma, which modern people find ourselves awash within, in various ways and in many locales across the planet. It's been said, and rightly so by my estimation, that depression itself – or the way we respond to it and caretake it - is a *failure of imagination.*

When I was growing up, as a student in public elementary schools, I remember the safety drills we were taught at the beginning of each school year. This was a time of great paranoia between America and Russia, at that time known as the Soviet Union. One of these exercises had us placing our huddled bodies underneath our study desks and tables listening to the emergency alarm on the loud-speakers in the event of a nuclear bomb attack. Even as children, we knew enough to understand that no simple school-desk was sturdy or solid enough to be able to save us from the effects of a nuclear explosion. How absurd does it get? After all, weren't those the kinds of bombs that could melt through steel walls and level entire cities, like Hiroshima? Television programs and other popular media at the time often depicted these issues and fears through fictional dramas, such as the memorable and jingoistic film *Red Dawn*.

Throughout the history of humankind, we can see how the ancestors of many living people today found themselves concerned over whether they would survive through the next blizzard, flood, drought, tsunami or earthquake. Uncertainty about the future, due to concerns about food, weather, shelter and clothing, must have been present on a daily basis amongst past tribes and various peoples – as they can be and still are today. Individually and collectively, humans have always been concerned with how to continue life for themselves, one another, for the animals and plants, lands, waters and airs that comprise the place called home.

It seems that during the modern era we have largely forgotten, along with our mythic understandings, that risk and adventure, endings and beginnings, dreams and imagination have always been a part of the making and receiving of life and death here on earth. In the "Age of Enlightenment" we've somehow grown arrogant enough to think that we could finally solve these issues through science, medicine and technology and leave them far behind. Now, the very creations we have hatched in these venues appear to be the ones that pose the greatest threat to our own, not to mention the planets, very survival and thrivance.

The reason that the Life-Death-Life cycle of death and
rebirth appears so often in our dreams and also in the world's
mythological narratives, is to remind us of these important and
vital threads of intelligence and understanding as they apply to and
influence everyday life and the soul. It may be that, only through
the authentic, genuine and honest engagement with our deepest and
truest soul practices and spiritual disciplines such as dream work,
incubation, meditation, vision seeking, storytelling, initiation and
so forth, will we be able to regain the kinds of imaginative and
creative abilities to see past and through the mistaken literalities of
the very viewpoints that we have clung to so tightly. It's as if
we've created a false sense of security in our vain attempt to stave
away the energies of transformation that are a necessary part of the
grief-soaked life we've been gifted with, as it is experienced here
on this beautiful yet endangered earth, where we might find
ourselves dreaming, wondering, questing, dying and living.

At the same time, if we only see certain situations, such as
death, as metaphoric and symbolic and misread what these forms
are, we might mistakenly assume that these energies aren't real.
They are actual too, according to their nature, and perhaps we need
to unfold our language to find ever-more accurate ways of
referring to, relating with, hosting and discussing the energies of
transformation, birth, death and rebirth. The symbolic and

metaphoric are actual also – they need not be understood as separate or distinct. My sense is that we'd also do well to recognize the differences and similarities between physical and psychic reality. Death, from the psyche's viewpoint, would seem to differ from death according to the body. At the same time, on some important level, psyche and body are also interwoven.

My trust is that by giving a wide berth to the energies of our dreams, our creative practices, story-carrying, music-making, painting and poetry, farming and dancing, and so much more, all of which can be seen and felt to emanate from a wise source within as well as without, we might apprentice ourselves to deep truths that are capable of reminding us about who and how we actually are, via learning experiences embraced within these disciplines. In this pursuit we might once again re-imagine ways of continuing that are inclusive of one another and the irreplaceable wild earth and all her growing-dying creatures and plants, this cosmos which is so excellent at caring for us amid the very real surprises and heartbreaks of a life fully lived.

What happens now is dearly vital to what comes next and also to sending an echo out that might be heard after the persons we are today cease to be. If we can live and die in an honorable and vital fashion, the people we may never meet, who follow behind us as we have followed those who have preceded our journeys, might find some value of profound worth and practical necessity in what we leave behind. The time to act on this is now.

Ultimately, to dream is to imagine, to make a contribution to the ongoing mystery of creation-destruction-creation. It has been my experience that dreams do reveal much wiser and deeper embodiments of belonging and being. Time and again I've witnessed dreamers who thought they were at a literal end – the end of intimacy, the end of their physical lives, the end of their known options for finding joy and fulfillment, the end of being able to bear the difficulties that attend our storied advents in this lifetime. I've seen these folks rediscover the thread of creative reality within the dreams and find ways to go on recreating a life worth living while also wrapping their arms around the actual endings of what has been, the grief that springs forth out of the waters of unavoidable pain which might yet become the nourishment and guidance for others as they follow along the way.

DREAMING OF DEATH,
THE BOONS OF PAYING ATTENTION

Incubation would seem to contain and emit the aroma of death, both symbolic and perhaps also literal. Dying may also be experienced as a kind of incubation – a hatching towards deep dreams.

I have witnessed countless dreams who have visited me and many others, that have made an apprenticeship to the actuality and symbolic resonance of dying and being reborn, as well as to attendant energies wrapped up in death.

In the early 2000's my father became ill with a form of lung cancer caused by a material that was used through the 1900's for insulation in construction – asbestos. I was privileged to be with him as he died. I was also fortunate to have received a tidal wave dream the night before his body went still and his spirit passed to the otherworld.

We didn't know each other very well, yet when news arrived that he was sick I knew I wanted to see him. It took me deciding to be in the thick of his dying time, a willingness for remaining open to "come what may", as well as many years of inner and outer work to be able to finally understand that my father didn't not like or disapprove of me, as I had always thought. Our perceptions of each other seemed to shift as we visited during the week prior to his death. I realized that really, all the explanations I had formed in my head about why he left when I was four years old didn't have as much to do with me as it did with who he was and who my mother was and how little they knew about how to be married and raise kids. That's the classic stuff of psychological wounding and its related history.

The point here is that I was alongside my dad when he died. I have never been with anyone else while they were dying. I'm currently forty-four years old. That this is the only human death I've witnessed seems like a massive oddity to me now. I've also never witnessed a human birth. How alive can we really be when the two defining bookends of our lives are so shrouded in secrecy and a medically, societally encoded detachment from what and who brings us here and what takes us out?

The dream I was visited by the morning that my father died was instructive, as well as predictive. That dream has created far-reaching influences, even years following the man's death. The nighttime vision seems quite simple:

I'm on the West coast at the beach. I know a big tidal wave is coming and that I have to warn my sister and my father about it as it will be here soon.

I don't quite know how I knew. But, I perceived the dream was warning me, my sister who I was staying with, and my dad to be on alert. Between the recalling of the dream and the time that my father started actually perceivably physically dying, I didn't have time to talk to him about it. That morning he didn't get out of bed. My sister received word from me over coffee to be ready for something big, like the wave in the dream.

Years later I read, in Ernest Hartman's book about nightmares, that it's quite common for death to be presaged in dreams in the form of tidal waves as a symbolic-actual energy. In our case, the dream, on one very crucial level, cleared the way for us to be available to dad while he "let go". That's my impression of how he looked and felt while dying – and it seemed to mysteriously and mystically imbue the space around and within all of us that morning.

Something about the whole experience was deeply healing. The night before he left his body, my father held my hand and we talked of sons and fathers. I can't tell you how meaningful and magnificent that felt to me – a son who always thought he didn't have a father finally found that he did. All in the midst of his death, which many never even agree to enter in an aware fashion in the first place, so I'm told. In the wake of his leave-taking, I learned that I could become more fully alive as a way of carrying him as one of my dead. This active understanding forms a kind of symbolic and real rebirth that I have continuously undergone in the intervening years as a result. In witnessing dad's death, it seemed quite apparent to both my sister and I that the man's spirit rose up and lifted out of his body. I can't prove it, but I have had many dreams over the years to suggest that he did "pass over" and that he's not gone or lost. He visits me in various forms in the

Dreaming from time to time. For that, I am so deeply grateful. His death wasn't for me, or my sister, not exclusively. It was for him and all of us - the rest of the family, for our family's families and for his community. It was and still is for a kind of remembrance – a putting back together again. His death took place for those who came before him and for those who will continue to come afterwards. I still hold and act out the beauty of the grief, which pours out of his death to this day and I'm seeking to do my part by telling his story here. I could write a whole book about it and maybe I will one day.

So, at least paying attention to the dreams, and at the most, asking for them to come to provide guidance and working with them, contemplating them and honoring them, can be a helpful and deeply instructive practice where death is concerned too. My sense, based on the work I've done with others and my own dreams, is that the dreams do gift us with a felt-sense and perceived awareness of the spiritual and soulful themes and experiences of life and death. They do connect us in unexpected, reliable fashions with "all of the above".

This all relates to incubation and dream work, in general, in that these are deeply, richly, archetypal practices that are inextricably bound up with the realities of birth, life, death, transformation, acceptance, suffering and rebirth. Each of these realities wend forth like threads composing the garment that we might help to weave, spun by the hands of culture and nature themselves. Anyone who honors their dreams, and seriously attends to them over a lengthy period will inevitably witness scenarios involving all of these vital and ever-present mythic inheritances, and more.

In this time and in this era, as in the moments that have led up to this age throughout the course of existence – and who really knows where and when it all began? – surprising alternatives capable of fostering life and meeting death have appeared and reappear in the visionary worlds of the dreaming imagination. The dream worlds bear a close relation and responsibility to the waking worlds of daily life too. The opportunity for us to dream our way through to the other side, and of becoming more fully alive here on the goat's green earth, may become more than apparent in working with the energies of true dreams, great stories and artful practices. We need only look as far as our own nightly sleep dreams and waking visionary forays for the clues, symbols and guidance that we can then apply to our waking manifestations of these instructive vitalities. In this pursuit, we may invoke the wisdom of our dreams for leading us into the unknown, stepping into our very own and the cosmos's mythical adventures as we do so, vulnerable, yet shining forth the beauty and wonder of the imaginative, soulful, spirited energies of the deeply creative and destructive powers that appear to be born, to die away and be rebirthed via the great mysterious and in the world, within and across many lifetimes and also throughout many dying times.

We do this work for the life and the death within, as well as without, apprenticing to the many forces that exist within and across the boundaries of many worlds and many realities, as Native American say, "For All Our Relations".

Endnotes Chapter 8

[1] Peter Kingsley, "In the Dark Places of Wisdom", 1999, The Golden Sufi Center, p 109

[2] Jeanne Achterberg, "Imagery in Healing, Shamanism and Modern Medicine", 1985, Shambala Publications, Boston, Massachusetts, p. 55-56

[3] Gayle Delaney, quoting Norman Mackenzie, "All About Your Dreams", 1998, Harper San Francisco, p.16, and, Norman Mackenzie, "Dreams and Dreaming", 1965, Vangaurd Press, New York, p. 31

[4] John Matthews, "Taliesen, Shamanism and the Bardic Mysteries in Britain and Ireland", 1991, The Aquarian Press, Harper Collins Publishers, p.57-58

[5] John Matthews, "The Celtic Shaman, A Practical Guide", 2001, Rider, an imprint of Ebury Press, Random House Publishing, p. 152-153

[6] C.G. Jung, "Dream Analysis", Edited by William McGuire, 1984, Princeton University Press, Princeton, New Jersey, p.179

[7] Lama Govinda, from the introductory forward, "The Tibetan Book of the Dead", "Bardo Thodol", Oxford University Press, London, 1976, p.1xii

Epilogue

During the writing of this work, which has gone on for the past six years, much learning has occurred. It's funny and sorrowful in our society. People tend to want to think that all that can be known is, and that it's all just a matter of adjustment and fine tuning at this point.

Could it be possible that there is no plateau where receiving (or offering) a real education is concerned? The word itself 'educare' refers to the drawing out of the inherent genius – the way I'm using it here, genius would mean, 'the guiding spirit'. Both places and people, and if it's not clear yet, the rest of creation-destruction contain such spirits who're alive *in this world*. When one wishes to refer to the guiding spirit of place, one could speak of the Genius Loci.

As I've been about the business of writing this book, I've been claimed by the notion that North American society has the tendency to make things "all about us". In the mainstream, nature admiration has become more of a form of pornography – look but don't touch. Psychology has either become a form of behavioral manipulation or medication taking. Spirituality feels mostly absent. The project of healing and becoming "self-aware" has had us seeking to grab, get and use the most beautiful forces of being and all the creatures that we cohabitate with on the terra firma for our own ends.

We could walk into a different mode now. I think some vigilance is called for around this and it seems readily visible that the *outward realms need us to be needed*, rather than to journal about or make pleas regarding our endless lists of "unmet needs". In this sense consciousness-raising involves recognizing that existence has to do with more than just "me, myself and I".

The practices presented here can, I think, help to open the borders and frontiers to a much wider recognition of what constitutes "us". Would we even be here if it weren't for countless myriad energies and hands, foods and waters that devotedly offer themselves up time and again, asking us to honor and pour a libation for them?

While nearing completion on *The Dreaming Well*, it occurred to me, thanks to one of my favorite piratical mythological writers and thinkers, how it's possible that stories from other shores may not feel so hot about being bandied around for the provenance of certain ideas. I've been struck by the teaching that a folk myth ought to be treated at least as respectfully as any two-legged visitor from afar.

So it is that I offer the following tale of my own effort to welcome the Skeleton Woman story to the small corner of the world in which I live.

BESEECHING A HOME FOR SKELETON WOMAN AND THE LONELY HUNTER

I'm heading off to the coast, having decided that it seems more than proper to ask the main story in this tome to willingly abide in the living terrain near my home. The devotion to this is also born out of a sense that an Inuit story may not be interested in relocating to a land further south than the one it was hatched within. After all, I am not myself an Inuit person and it seems deeply fitting to do everything I can to pay my respects, ask permission to create relation, and seek to do so *with style*.

It's an autumn midafternoon, unseasonably warm and I aim my Honda Element through the backroads toward nearby Doran Beach. The inner pace is too rushed. I'm nervous and feel a deep responsibility to the task. Just before reaching Bodega Highway seems like a good spot to pull over and offer a petition. Hands go up in the Celtic prayer position and requests are made to bring honor and authenticity to the moment and the undertaking.

Feeling much more grounded and slowed down, I take the turn off to my right and realize the stop will slow me down in more ways than one. There's a truck in front of me loaded up with what at first appear to be some sort of containers headed off to the recycling. A closer look reveals that in fact, the flatbed in front of me is piled with crabbing cages. Well now – that'll do for an encouraging sign! The journey proceeds and I can't help but to smile at the fact of being behind a waking life hunter-fisherman with his or her tackle bundled up in front of my very eyes.

People at the beach are in shorts and tank tops. The wispy fanning clouds are mist-laden in the skies and it's balmy. The shoes come off and the hand-woven medicine bag replete with raven flute, chocolate, whiskey and fresh sardines for the offering in the hearth to be made all come along with me. I've dressed up for the date, though I don't think I'll need my buckskin jacket. It's a real beauty and I always look for chances to wear it even though it almost always feels too much; it was made from deer-skin by a Native man named Douglas Mountain Dreamer for my Dad, and I inherited it when he died.

The old guys and mentors that I know who have tried to teach how to carry out the endeavor that is now unfolding have said that there is much to be made in the *approach* to the sacred. A pause is made at the place where earth meets sand and further out roiling sea. The raven flute comes forth and a song of querying lofts on the wind. Is there permission to enter? A seagull circles round from left to right and settles near some seaweed over the berm. Doesn't quite convince. Breaths continue to waft through the handmade native flute and in a few moments a whole mob of starlings alight from behind and over my right shoulder before gathering up on the beach, feet away. That's sensed as a clear come hither.

The sand feels like an old friend's company to my naked feet. I stroll down the strand keeping eyes, ears and heart open for other omens as I walk southward. Soon, the vision of a skeleton gull meets my curiosity. It's almost fully picked clean and utterly wound up in a freshly beached brew of sea grass. An offering is made to the little daughters and sons and I move on.

Now nervousness returns again. The stakes feel high – the spot I find and the telling of the story are both important moves in the courting of the tale. To build a home for the story, a sheltered spot seems key – at the same time, there's an awareness of the tearing down and the rebuilding in the story that wants to be honored too.

Off past what must be a couple hundred years old piece of massive and sunken in driftwood, there's some scrappy looking pines and scrub bush nearby that holds promise. Settling in, I do my best jaybird impersonation and go for a dunk a safe distance from the formidable breakers. The day is so warm and I can hardly believe it's possible to get an easy soak in early November. Remembrance of the imagining of that time beneath the mighty waters comes rolling over with each wave and when I feel entered by and held within the ocean I crawl out. The sun will go into the Underworld in about an hour. Time to craft the sea hut and offer my offering of the tale.

I set up a very humble and small lean-to and pour some Jameson as libation. The sardines, chocolate, dried turkey and sage are all next to the hearth. The telling is brought up and out.

The story sinks in when I feel that swaying once more and actually can sense the little daughter going down and being eaten. Next comes the fright and the mad journey back to the snow hut. I'm feeling every ounce of that fear, and then the tenderness and the re-enfleshment of the skeleton woman casts a visceral flavor in both stomach and thighs. Whilst singing, a light breeze carries the voice and there's palpable flavor of some form of visitation. "The whole engagement is not for me or for what I can get out of it", I keep reminding myself, more so, there's a returning to how this is for the living person of the story himself and herself.

There's a solid impression at the end, yet also an "is it really finished" quality. Whatever happens now is between the story and the place that I've told it. So I have it, on good authority. The effort is so fledgling and raw. No less, a pledge is made to go on carrying the story and to also pay attention to up-coming dreams for any messages and indications that the work has been well-made.

Sleep comes easy back at the rabbit farm in the redwoods and thanks are given for being brought into such an attempt, to the beach, distant mentors, myriad elements, animals and plant people and the storied energies encountered.

To date, I'm not sure if the story has accepted the home which was so humbly crafted. Soon I'll go out to the beach again to see if there's any clues as to whether or not there might be a good match.

I can say that there've been some intriguing dreams about old-time wooden sushi restaurants built by close friends that have piqued a sense of wonderment. What happens next will be a story for some other time. Until then...

...here's to the dreamsongs and dreaming stories and seeking to continue learning for the sake of a much wider family.

With that I leave you now amid the notes of the following romantic era poem from Holderlin. I trust the poetic to spin together any loose threads that may be lingering.

Bread and Wine Part 7

Oh Friend, we arrived too late. The divine energies
Are still alive, but isolated above us, in the archetypal world.

They keep on going there, and apparently, don't bother if
Humans live or not... that is a heavenly mercy.

Sometimes a human's clay is not strong enough to take the water;
Human beings can carry the divine only sometimes.

What is living now? Night dreams of them. But craziness
Helps, so does sleep, Grief and Night toughen us,
Until people capable of sacrifice once more rock
In the iron cradle, desire people, like the ancients, strong enough for
water.

In thunderstorms it will arrive. I have the feeling often, meanwhile,
It is better to sleep, since the Guest comes so seldom;

We waste our life waiting, and I haven't the faintest idea
How to act or talk... in the lean years who needs poets?

But poets as you say are like the holy disciple of the Wild One
Who used to stroll over the fields through the whole divine night.

Friedrich Holderlin, translated by Robert Bly

Let's also raise a glass to the Wild Ones once more strolling amongst us
here and now and give a real hoot for that.

Blessed Be, Travis Wernet, Occidental California, November 2016

www.ingramcontent.com/pod-product-compliance
Lightning Source LLC
Chambersburg PA
CBHW060837280326
41934CB00007B/815